HARVARD UNIVERSITY GRADUATE SCHOOL OF DESIGN

STUDIO WORKS 4

approaches

Editors

Brooke Hodge
*Director of Lectures, Exhibitions,
and Academic Publications*

Linda Pollak
Assistant Professor of Architecture

Student Editors

Jay Berman
MArch '98

Rose Brady
MLA '96

Dean, Faculty of Design
Peter G. Rowe

Copyright © 1996 President and Fellows of Harvard College

Library of Congress Catalog Card Number 96-80352
International Standard Book Number 1-56898-100-7

Published by Harvard University Graduate School of Design
Distributed in the United States of America by Princeton Architectural Press

Printed in the United States of America

Copies of *Studio Works 4* are available for purchase from:

Harvard University Graduate School of Design
Book Orders
48 Quincy Street
Cambridge, MA 02138
617. 496. 5113

Table of Contents

Dean's Prologue

The aim of this issue of *Studio Works,* as in the past, is to capture the essential character of the design studio experience at the Graduate School of Design. In short, it provides a snapshot of a year in the life of design students at Harvard, and an archive of their design speculations and deliberations. This year's theme is the pedagogy of design studio instruction, and in the following pages, alternative approaches are highlighted and discussed.

Studios at the Graduate School of Design vary in format. There are workshops quickly emphasizing experience with difficult design conditions and emphasizing the acquisition of specific design skills. These tend to be a part of the introductory or 'core' studio programs. There are also semester-long design problems, with or without an internal sequence of separate exercises, and there are studios which are media constrained, emphasizing specific representational techniques or technologies, like computer imaging. Some studios are also sponsored from the outside, affording students and faculty the chance to travel and experience remote sites and gain valuable first-hand contact with the actual participants in a design situation. For some time now the Graduate School of Design has been running sponsored studios in a broad range of international contexts from Europe to Asia, Africa and Latin America. Here the breadth of cultural experience is invaluable, allowing all concerned to question their underlying assumptions about the design world. Indeed, sponsored studios are one of the consistently distinctive and notable aspects of the studio program at Harvard, especially at the 'options level,' beyond the initial 'core' studio program.

Regardless of differences in format, all studios have a specific focus. No attempt is made to comprehensively simulate office practice. Rather all studios operate within a pedagogical framework with specific educational, as distinct from strictly professional, ends. To make an analogy with certain ideas about science, the explicitly speculative nature of design studios make them rather more especial than simply normal or routine in their focal interests. Here advantage is also taken of a strong and broadly-based program of visiting critics—another hallmark of the studio experience at the Graduate School of Design. These advantages include an added breadth of perspective, different styles of studio instruction and a widened design outlook.

Peter G. Rowe
Dean, Faculty of Design

Editorial Statements

This publication presents just a fragment of the work that has been produced in studios at the GSD during the past year. A reader can interpret this material on many levels. Each image or group of images represents a project. A project implies accompanying drawings and models, verbal presentation, critical discussion, and a history of development over the course of the semester, in relation to technical, social, and aesthetic issues. What do the hundreds of images in this volume say about design education? How do they convey a new generation's approaches to design? What kinds of evidence do they provide of tools, thinking processes, and criteria?

Since its inception, *Studio Works* has emphasized the means of design studio as well as its ends, in response to Dean Peter Rowe's desire to present the life of the school in studio in a way that is timebound and specific. In addition to serving constituencies beyond the GSD, the publication is a place where the School can look at itself—where each of us has the opportunity to penetrate places that do not easily reveal themselves, in spite of their proximity in a single open studio space.

Studio Works has proven to be a useful vehicle for exploring relationships within the school. The previous issue's focus on boundaries demonstrated that putting the departments together, whether in this publication or in studio, does not necessarily create a synthesis; the function of the four-year-old Universal Studio Lottery is not to produce universality. As that issue's Student Discussion demonstrated, provocative things can happen as unlikely neighbors inform each others' search for conceptual tools.

This volume's focus on Approaches recognizes how large the School is, and how much goes on here. In a global climate of increasing homogenization, the GSD's vitality comes partly from the fact that its long-embedded differences are no longer accepted without question. Rather, noticed and valued, these differences are becoming vital places of exchange. Specifically, Approaches begins from the premise that differences of approach within a department can be as substantial as those between departments. We have attempted to bring forward differences in pedagogy and design work that are not necessarily attached to disciplinary categories, nor always evident when looking at images of work.

During our fourth year of editing this publication, Brooke Hodge and I have noted some tendencies in and across the studio work itself, that I want to point out, and offer some interpretation of. There tends to be a lot of generalization about studio, yet the diversity of studio work reveals the futility of generalities when trying to think through issues associated with teaching design. These days, there is no such thing as a typical studio. In a time of evolving social and ecological concerns, of vastly increased representational capabilities offered by computers, and of numerous other forces that have impacted on intellectual, technical, and economic aspects of design, each studio is in some way stretching established parameters.

As a project-based advanced education, studio is neither expedient, economical, nor efficient. This burden of unwieldiness is not a surface flaw. It is basic to the teaching of design. In order to function within this challenging environment, it is vital that faculty from within and beyond studio, along with visiting critics and students, share a level of understanding of its possibilities and limitations. Yet this kind of understanding is the exception rather than the rule. We hope that the specificities of this volume will break through some of the studio mystique, and contribute to a richer understanding of what goes on.

In "Theory and the Design Studio," faculty members from several departments focus on questions of the relationship between design teaching and design theory. While this particular conversation was initiated by the Student Editors, the topic has been a recurrent focus at the School recently. Discussions such as this one are important to establish an understanding of parameters at a departmental or institutional level. From the perspective of studio, the debate about theory can be seen as a debate about conceptual tools. The fact that the tools of the disciplines vary from one another is not a function of the fixed identity of any discipline, but exists in dynamic relation to asthetic, technical, and human concerns. Because the limits of understanding are not set by a dominant ideal, the role of theory in design studio is inseparable from the definition of design: one critic may regard design as real-world problem solving, while another might frame it as creative redefinition of a problem, and a third might take a purely aesthetic approach, that avoids real-world problems altogether.

The use of built artifacts as material for research and interpretation connects some of the most diverse pedagogies at the school. And it would seem that here if anywhere, in the context of concrete conditions, lies objective fact. Yet the selection of artifacts and the determination of modes of research constitute basic differences. Students in one studio may begin from and work intimately with a single building for an entire semester. Another studio may implement existing projects as typological precedents. Analytical techniques might be formally based or not, might include or exclude an awareness of the artifact's historical circumstances, might rely heavily on writing or not at all. And so on.

Another thing that is commonly said about studio is that it is distant from the real world. But the nature and size of this distance depends on the approach of the critic, as well as the definition of reality. Some of the complexities involved in bridging this distance emerge in the "Bronzeville Roundtable," which included participants from the first two semesters of the Bronzeville Studio taught by Lee Cott. As the students' discussion reveals, some aspects of the real world are resistant to the limitations of a studio semester, yet possibilities can emerge from even partial successes.

We are fortunate to have some of the Studio Options critics from the past year, including Cott, articulate their own approaches to design work and teaching. These provocative essays link approaches to design with philosophical, practical, and aesthetic issues. Each one, presented alongside the work of the studio, addresses questions of pedagogy that often go unremarked. Pierre David frames the design of new cities as a search for place within the mapping of a landscape; Wilfried Wang critically reexamines and rejects the Master Class concept; Chris Risher proposes "shapely form" as a liberating response to the authority of structure; Lee Cott and Carl Steinitz both address issues related to practice: Cott's text communicates the agility required by a pedagogical approach that moves outside of the institution; Steinitz discusses the need to train "conductors" as well as "soloists." Sandro Marpillero describes how he initiates a studio by establishing a tension between urban analysis and "techniques of invention" derived from surrealism and psychoanalytic thought; Larry Mitnick meditates on architecture's contact with reality; and Carlos Jimenez articulates his commitment to help students to discover architecture as a cultural force. In their specificity, these eight texts suggest the range of approaches within the more than thirty studio options offered in the past year.

The question of approaches is equally relevant in core studios. In the second year of the architecture program, or in Urban Design's first semester of Elements, class size means that six or seven critics teach the "same" project. It would be naive to maintain a pretense of homogeneity under these circumstances. Cohesion is critical, but where does it come from? The necessity to construct a shared language, as well as to acknowledge criteria other than one's own, is fundamental to the core studio process.

While the same issues are integrated in all sections of a studio semester, a shift in emphasis can radically alter their meaning. One studio may stress the impact of construction, another may focus on processes of transformation within a typological approach, and social concerns may define the framework of a third. A shared review might take advantage of issues revealed by one section's sketch problem on communal spaces, and another group's research into implications of code issues.

Each studio is a testing ground—a unique critical territory that presents investigative opportunities. Success resides in establishing a dynamic relation between the studio's focus and each student's evolving strengths and inclinations. Students build their own approach as they move from one studio to the next. Depending on the program, the accumulation of these investigations leads to a thesis, where a student develops his or her position through the formulation of a design problem as well as a project. Experience with different pedagogies helps students develop a self-critical awareness as they pursue their individual design research.

It is a daunting task to put together this volume, which includes the work of so many individuals, and represents many more. We hope that the arrangement of these diverse visual and verbal materials allows them to support each other, and facilitates their interpretation.

Linda Pollak
Assistant Professor of Architecture

A wise design student recognizes relationships between one semester's studio project and the last, and predicts issues and interests for exploration in the next; each project stands on its own as well as within a body of work. So with *Studio Works 4* we acknowledge the previous three volumes and anticipate *Studio Works 5*. As each issue is its own project, marking the thoughts, mood, and spirit of the Graduate School of Design in a particular year, a series of *Studio Works* charts a roadmap of design thought and education at the GSD over time. Yet, while each issue is its own undertaking, it is not its own end. *Studio Works* exists in relation to the work it contains, and as a contribution to, as well as a product of, the institution of which it is a part.

Studio Works' challenge is not just to represent, but to engage, inform, interrogate, and most of all, to participate. In this evolving role, previous volumes have used essays, dialogues, interviews, and roundtable discussions as links between studio and broader issues such as the relationship between theory and practice, and the interdisciplinary nature of design education and the design professions.

Studio Works 4 focuses on the studio itself, so to speak, devising a framework in which images of student work and essays and discussions comment directly on one another. With the goal of allowing studio work to generate the publication, we have operated under the broad rubric of Approaches.

The idea of approaches provides both a way to break down the complexity, wealth, and diversity of work and a structure for putting things back together in printed form. It is also a lens through which readers can engage images and writing on these pages as instances of individual thought and creativity as well as reflections of the diverse and energetic spirit of inquiry and production at the GSD.

Eight essays written by studio options critics explore their own particular approaches, with emphasis on the evolution of the studio work itself. These essays effectively dismiss the notion that studio work can be seen as a static body and highlight the dynamic nature of the relationship between critic, program, and student.

The "Bronzeville Roundtable" brings together students from two urban design studios taught in the fall and spring semesters. Bronzeville I and Bronzeville II examined and made proposals for the Bronzeville neighborhood on Chicago's South Side. Discussion highlighted questions of approach implied by the nature of the project, the goals of the critic, and the experiences of the students. Such issues as confronting inner-city problems, operating in a public setting, working in teams, student and client interaction, and methods of representation and presentation provide a glimpse into the interrelationship of approaches and the proceedings of a particular studio.

"Theory and The Design Studio" assembles faculty to discuss the role of theory in relation to studio. Whether theory constitutes an approach itself, if it can constitute the substance of or more modestly inform a studio, the idea that theory might be instrumentalized or implicit, its relationship to practice, and distinctions between theory we speak of in studio and Theory as a discipline itself were among topics encountered in a far-reaching and provocative conversation at the GSD one afternoon in June, 1996.

We have endeavored to animate discussions, to make essays speak, and to make design work stand on these pages as substantially as it does on the desks and walls of the GSD.

Jay Berman MArch '98
Rose Brady MLA '96

Introduction to the Departments

Architecture

For generations, Harvard has educated men and women who have assumed major leadership roles in shaping the built environment. Today's graduates continue this tradition by answering the demanding challenges posed by contemporary society. Architects draw upon knowledge and experience gained from the past while adapting to the changing needs of the modern world. Some roles played by the architect remain the same, but new ways of thinking and working in the profession have emerged; the School remains vigilant to this evolution, understanding that demands on design grow increasingly complex and require new interpretations.

The selection of work by students in the Department of Architecture, shown in *Studio Works 4*, represents the varied pedagogical objectives of the department's sequential studio structure. Each studio experience — from core studios to studio options and, finally, to the independent design thesis — is an opportunity for the distillation and synthesis of the complex and far-reaching issues that define architecture.

The four-semester-long core sequence progresses from the design of small projects with limited scope and narrowly focused objectives through larger and more complex projects with ambitious urban intentions that engage, through architecture, a broad range of sociocultural and physical concerns. The studio options, offered in conjunction those of the Departments of Landscape Architecture and Urban Planning and Design, provide students with the opportunity to explore architecture through a diversity of issues, scales, technologies, and critical positions. The thesis program, in which each student works with an advisor from the faculty, promotes and enables significant individual research in design. At all levels of studio instruction, students and faculty are encouraged to establish and open-ended discourse about the possibilities of contemporary architecture.

It is the commitment of the Department of Architecture to focus our academic and pedagogical agendas on the larger social issues that architecture must address both today and for the next century.

Jorge Silvetti, *Chair*
Nelson Robinson, Jr., Professor of Architecture

Landscape Architecture

The works of landscape architecture are broad in scale and scope, ranging from the design of parks and gardens to the ecological planning of large tracts of land. Landscape architects share a commitment to the creative application of design and technology and to ensuring ecological appropriateness and social responsibility in their work with the landscape. With the continuing expansion of our cities and suburban areas, landscape architects increasingly become not only the designers of new landscapes, but also the advocates of landscape rescue and conservation. As such, landscape architects are called upon to create landscapes that respond to the broad range of human habitation in diverse cultural and ecological contexts. The creative fulfillment of these responsibilities can become an absorbing, lifelong career.

At Harvard the design studio provides the core of learning and inquiry. Instruction and research in the design studios emphasize transformation, critical analysis, and synthetic inclusion of visual studies, theory, history, and scientific research. Design instruction in the department fosters invention and creativity, while also cultivating the skills required for informed decision-making. As part of the production of each new landscape, students are encouraged to draw from historical precedents, art, design theory, civil engineering, site analysis, and most importantly from their imagination. The educational experience of landscape architecture students is further enriched by interactions with the departments of Architecture, Urban Planning and Design, the Fogg Art Museum, the Arnold Arboretum, Harvard Forest, Dumbarton Oaks in Washington D.C., and other resources in the New England area. Cross-cultural and multidisciplinary perspectives on design problems and practices are offered by visiting faculty from other countries and from other professional backgrounds.

Michael Van Valkenburgh, *Chair*
Professor in Practice of Landscape Architecture

Urban Planning and Design

The department of Urban Design and Planning brings together scholars and professionals who address the critical and complex conditions of modern cities and towns. In addition to design, faculty specialties and courses of instruction encompass legal, socioeconomic, environmental, historical, and aesthetic influences on urban planning and design. Students in the urban design programs address problems of increasing development in the suburbs, the decaying structure of older cities, and urban expansion in countries throughout the world. They are charged with the responsibility for shaping future development to meet social, economic, and cultural needs, while preserving and enhancing those aspects of urban form that have enduring value. In mastering the roles of urban planners and designers, GSD students learn to apply their knowledge of social values and historic precedents, along with their design skills, to urban conditions. Particular emphasis is placed on inquiry, speculation, and practice through design studio offerings and the pursuit of individual thesis projects

The studio sequence begins with Elements of Urban Design, a core offering required of all incoming urban planning and design students. The focus of this studio is on interpretation and representation of city form. A variety of studio options follows, each with a different orientation. Collectively, they attempt to expose students to a broad range of urban design situations.

The studio options offered each term address theoretical and pragmatic issues pertinent to the planning and design of cities in the US and abroad. Sited in varied cultural contexts, they offer an opportunity to explore a range of public and private interventions. Studios sponsored by donors allow field trips to the sites. This year students traveled to Athens, Greece; Chicago, Illinois; Gdansk, Poland; New York City; and Singapore.

The independent thesis gives students an opportunity to explore topics of their own interest. These topics vary in scope and include design demonstrations of urban design principles and concepts, abstract design explorations into theoretical issues of interest, and academic studies of a theoretical or historical nature.

François Vigier, *Chair*
Charles Dyer Norton Professor of Regional Planning

CORE STUDIOS

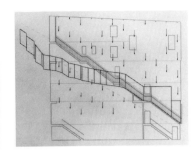

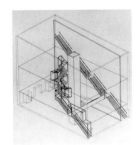

Matthew LaRue MArch '99, Elevator Intervention

Introduction to Design and Visual Studies in Architecture

Scott Cohen, *coordinator*
Darell Fields
Jeffrey Inaba
Lisa Iwamoto
Luis Rojo de Castro
James Williamson

Drawings and buildings are the two primary media by which architecture is made manifest. They are never identical and they always elude the other indispensable medium of architectural description: the word. Whether combined or separated, these media lack the descriptive range required to fully account for architecture. Architecture, as a symbolic construct that configures our perceptual and social spaces, always exceeds the depictions that make it physical.

During the first semester, projects concentrated on the complex relationship between particular built and drawn representations of architecture. What are the technical and conceptual problems that emerge when distinct manifestations of architecture are intended to approximate one another? The first project, "survey and analysis," required students to capture and dissect the space and materials of existing buildings within the space and ephemerality of orthographic drawings. The requirement to create a likeness between three-dimensional space and its two-dimensional representation encouraged acute awareness of fundamental tools and tasks of the architect's craft; in this case, intense observation and exacting formal definition became imperative.

The second project asked students to reverse the process of the first by interpreting a set of drawings of an existing building as a three-dimensional context for the intervention of an elevator. The building's dynamic section was so tightly calibrated with alternating centralized and bifurcated plans that the intervention of a continuous vertical passage, no matter how well integrated on any given level, would inevitably interrupt a room, stair, or passage on another level. The problem was to absorb the elevator and to reestablish the rigorous formal coherence and connectivity of the existing configuration while attending to implicit customs of sequence and occupation. In the second stage of the project, the building was assumed to be re-situated 90 degrees with respect to its street address. The problem, to readjust the plan, section, and elevations of the building to address a different front, required the renegotiation and redeployment of compositional and combinatory rules recovered during the elevator intervention.

The last project, a recreation center, introduced program as an explicit source of formal determination. In this case, basketball, squash, bowling, and batting became the progenitors of arrangements and residual spaces analogous to those of the previous projects. The challenge was to design a building that conglomerated the inherently determined sizes, proportions, axes of orientation, materials, fenestration, structural spans, and other pressures of the various recreational volumes within the limiting boundaries of an urban site. During the development of the project, critical focus was given to the configurative and derivational logics of the programmatic constituents and the urban context as well as to their anticipated symbolic and experiential resonance.

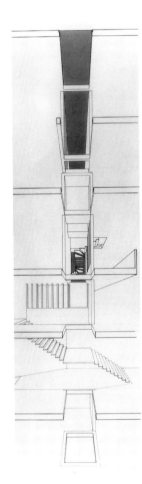

Nicolas Keleman MArch '99,
Elevator Intervention

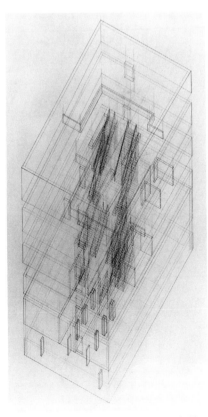

Annegret Schaible MArch '99, Axonometric View
of Elevator Intervention

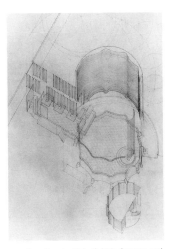

Ben Russin MArch '99, Survey and
Analysis, Kresge Chapel, MIT

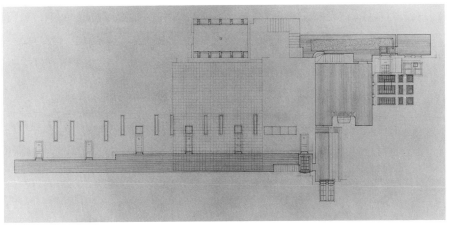

Christina Long MArch '99, Survey and Analysis, Linden Street Squash Courts

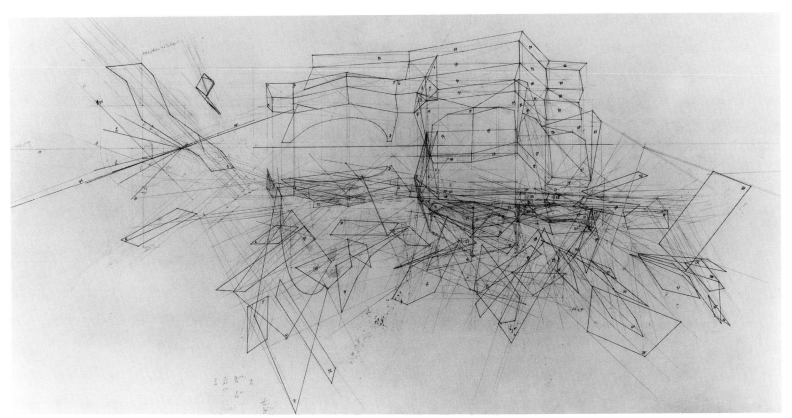

Likit Kittisakdinan MArch '99, Index Model Working Drawing

Zeke Brown MArch '99, Conceptual Model

Michael Weissman Bardin MArch '99, Survey
and Analysis, Austin Hall

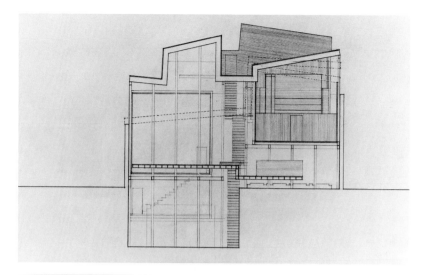

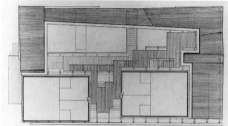

Christina Long MArch '99, Section and Plan
of Recreation Center

Plan, Section, and Perspective View

Christian Daag MArch '99, Model View of Recreation Center

Kwan Kim MArch '99, Model View of
Recreation Center

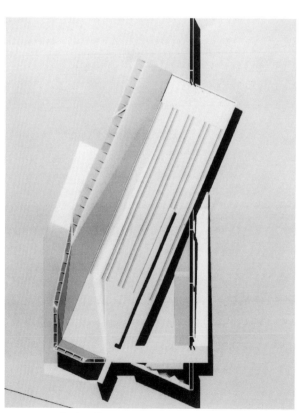

Ho-San Chang MArch '99, Renderings of Recreation Center

Pavlina Lucas MArch '99, Model View:
Dormitory for City Year Program

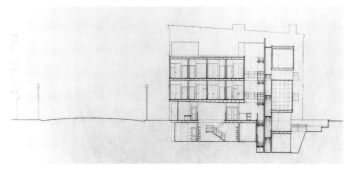

Sang Lee MArch '99, Longitudinal Section: Dormitory for City Year Program

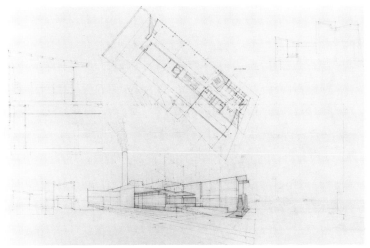

Christian Daag MArch '99, Perspective View and Plan: Furniture Gallery and Workshop

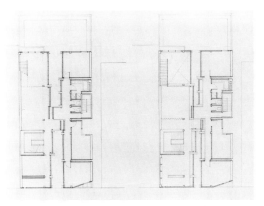

Eugene Park MArch '99, Plans for City Year
Program Dormitory

Introduction to Design and Visual Studies in Architecture

Silvia Acosta
Jeffrey Inaba
Jude LeBlanc, *coordinator*
Jonathan Levi
Monica Ponce de Leon
Peter Wiederspahn

The primary purpose of the second semester is to continue the introduction of basic architectural concepts—space, structure, use, and context—begun in the first semester, while working toward a more complex synthesis between them.

Two projects were assigned in order to develop methods for design and spatial analysis. The first project was a dormitory for the community–based City Year program in Boston and the second was a facility, located in Cambridge, for the design, production, and exhibition of furniture.

The compressed site of the City Year project suggested an investigation of section while the furniture production facility foregrounded issues of site planning.

In both cases the containing structure of the city provoked students to address issues of context and site as integral to design proposals. Analysis began with careful study of the respective programs and sites, while an emphasis was placed on connections between spatial articulation and constructional clarity.

Studio explorations were enhanced by a strategic parallel with the sequence of topics introduced in the required technology course, Building Construction. The first design project stipulated wood-frame construction and the second project necessitated long-span or point-load construction. This meant that case studies selected for analysis in the construction course had direct relevance to design studio, thereby promoting a synthesis between construction and design and between analysis and design.

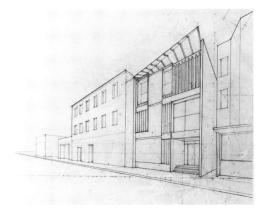

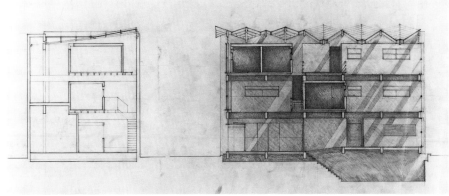

Kwan Kim MArch '99, Perspective View and Sections: Dormitory for City Year Program

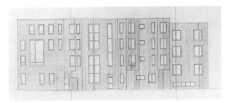

Uwrapped Elevation

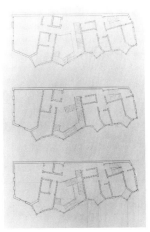

Lindsay Smith MArch '99, Plans
for City Year Dormitory

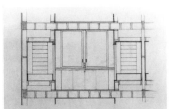

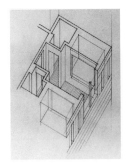

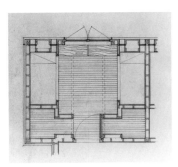

Matthew LaRue MArch '99, Plan, Section, and Axonometric
View of Dormitory Room for City Year

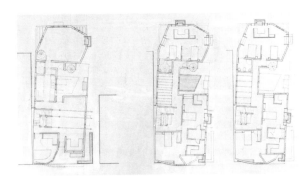

Plans

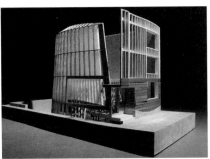

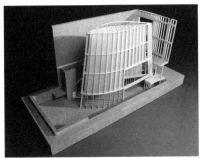

Malcolm Berg MArch '99, Model Views: Furniture Gallery and Workshop

Ann Bergren MArch '99, Conceptual Model for City Year Dormitory

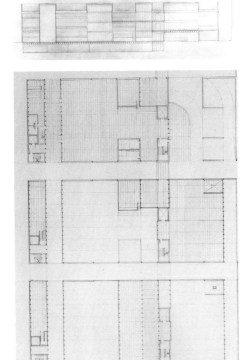

Gullivar Shepard MArch '99, Plans and Section:
Furniture Gallery and Workshop

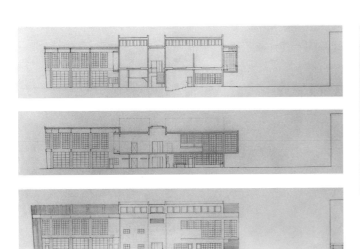

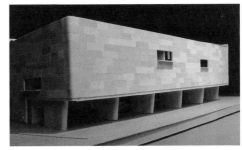

Joshua Comaroff MArch '99, Model View: Furniture Gallery and Workshop

Joshua Fenollosa MArch '99, Section/Elevations and Perspective View: Furniture Gallery and Workshop

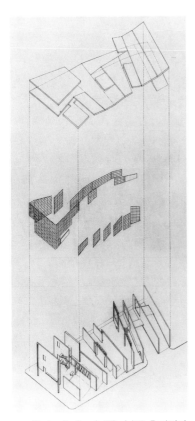

Zeke Brown MArch '99, Model View: Furniture Gallery and Workshop

Marion Drobnack MArch '99, Exploded Analytical Axonometric and Interior Perspective View: Furniture Gallery & Workshop

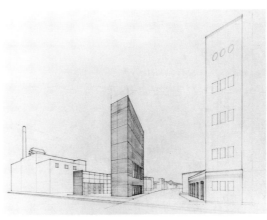
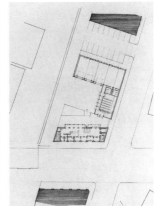

Joel Schmidt MArch '99, Plan and Perspective View: Furniture Gallery and Workshop

Annegret Schaible MArch '99, Partial Model: Furniture Gallery and Workshop

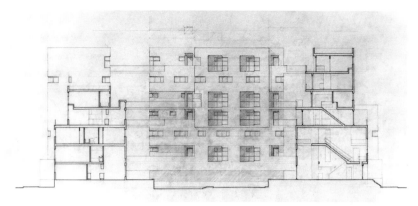

Study Model of Townhouse Unit

Jay Berman MArch '98, Site Section/Elevation

Design of Housing/ Relationships of Scale

George Baird, *coordinator*
Sheila Kennedy
Jude LeBlanc
Jonathan Levi
Toshiko Mori
Monica Ponce de Leon

The third semester core studio is conceived as a semester-long research in housing. The notion of scale affords a thematic study of relationships aimed toward understanding how design thinking establishes structural similarities among diverse artifacts, as well as how these are related to larger conceptual and physical contexts.

Methodologically, the curriculum establishes relationships between analysis and design as necessarily linked and reiterative. Three design briefs described distinct yet interrelated design studies: the first one documented and analyzed an excellent canonical example of housing design; the second one used this documentation and analysis as a site for intervention within the form of the canonical example, based on social practices which vary from those operative at the time of its creation. Finally, the third one called for a housing program to be devised and designed for a particular site. The choice of site was a major issue, intended to further frame the studio problem. Located on Washington Street in the South End neighborhood of Boston, the site was a full block of a rather complex kind, with very distinct scales and types of buildings and open spaces on each of the blocks abutting it.

Within third semester core, the question of site has been identified as a fundamental issue for the continuing development of the curriculum of this studio. A specific location provides a particular conceptual and physical matrix for housing: with equal importance, specific locations can characterize distinct forms of urbanity for study by students and critics together.

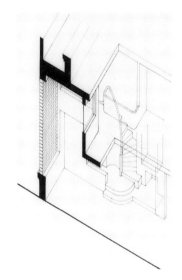

Precedent Analysis

Sarah Radding MArch '98, Washington Street Elevation

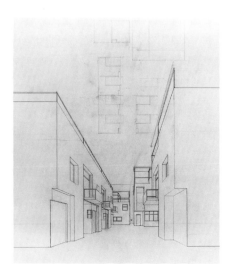

Caroline Hu MArch '98, Interior Block Perspective

Model View

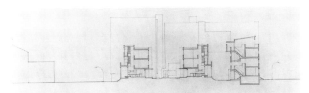

Hiromi Hosoya MArch '98, Site Section and Model View

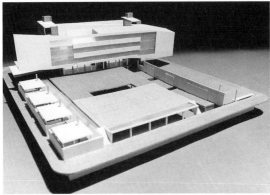

Mark Careaga MArch '98, Model Views

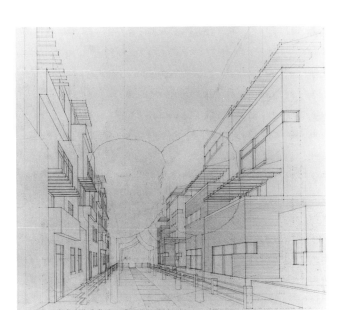

David Burnett MArch '98, Perspective View

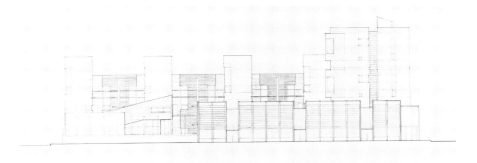

Elevation

Model View

Tran Vinh MArch '98, Site Plan

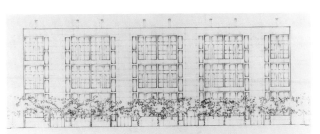

Christy Collins MArch '98, Elevation

Perspective View and Analytical Drawings

Elizabeth Whittaker MArch '98, Section

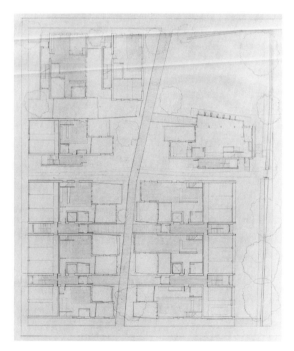

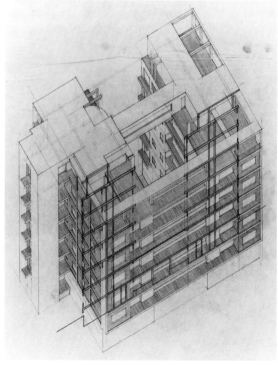

Axonometric View

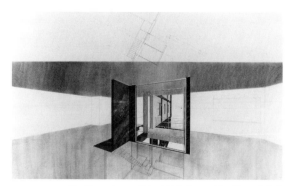

Sze Tsung Leong MArch '98, Perspective View of Unit

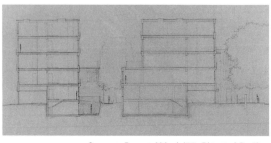

Suzanne Bowers MArch '98, Plan and Section

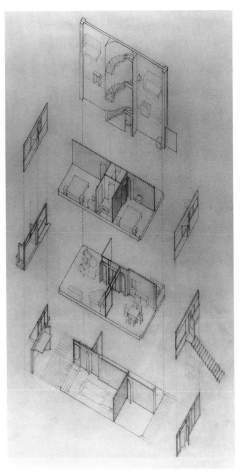

Site Plan

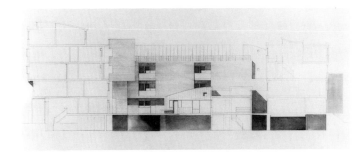

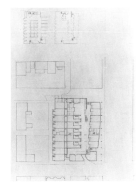

Markus Schaefer MArch '98,
Site Section/Elevation
and Site Plan

Alexandra Barker MArch '98, Analysis of Precedent:
Drive-in Flats

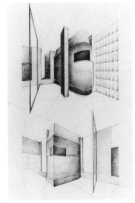

Perspective Views

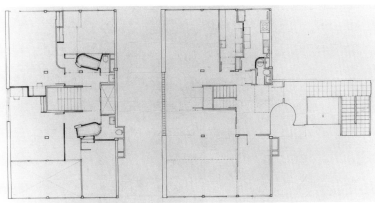

Michael Lin MArch '98, Plans: Intervention

Takashi Yanai MArch '98, Model View

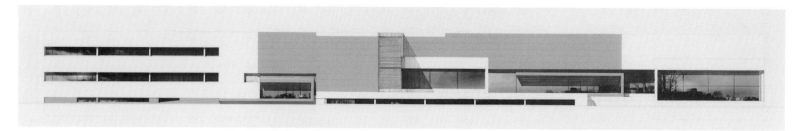

Sze Tsung Leong MArch '98, Elevation

Public Space as Public School (and/or vice versa)

Scott Cohen
Homa Fardjadi
Darell Fields, *coordinator*
Mark Linder
Linda Pollak
James Williamson

The development of a public school in relation to various conceptual realities of the city (Boston) was the focal point of proposed strategies and interventions for this semester. The programmatic identity of the school as working on and in the city was understood both as an internalization of urbanity and as an extension of a (so-called) public institution. Through the simultaneous disruption of their respective similarities and differences, both city and school were reinvented as "civic spatial institutions." The catalyst of this reinvention was engaged from the very start. It is the moment that the student realized that the "publicness" of the school did not signify the same "publicness" of the city. Here, the terms public (public school) and public (public space or realm) are more than different—they are oppositional. If continued to be held apart, these publics can only produce synthetic realities. However, by using architecture to sustain (rather than conceal) the inherent conflict between these institutions, students were more capable of calibrating the intended civic meaning existing between city and school.

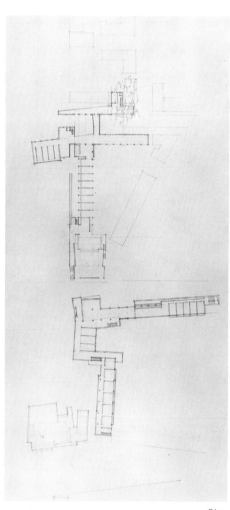

Plan

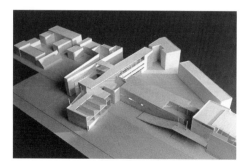

Hiromi Hosoya MArch '98, Model View

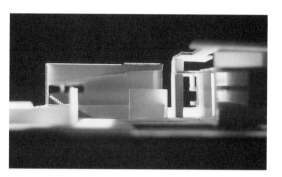

Michael Samra MArch '98, Model Views

Analysis Drawings of Ruggles Site

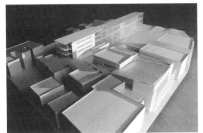

Daniel Monti MArch '98, Model Views

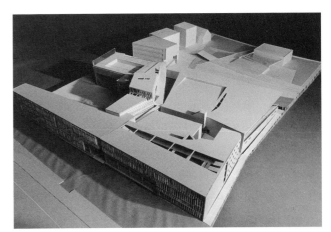

Kiwa Matsushita MArch '98, Model View

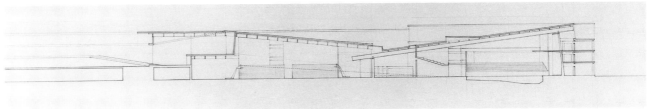

Michael Lin MArch '98, Section

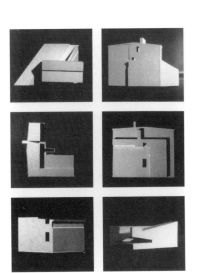

Susanna Woo MArch '98, 'Linguistic' Analytical Models

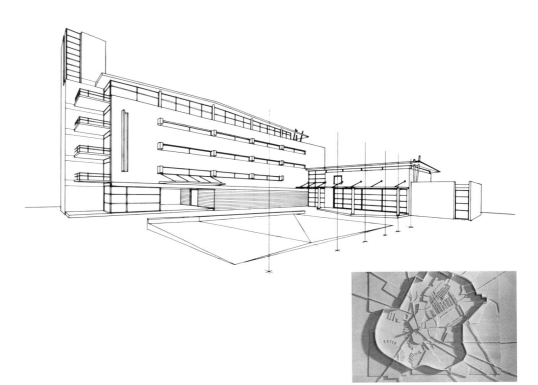

Ming-Yuan Wang MArch '98
Perspective View and Relief Model
of Ruggles Site

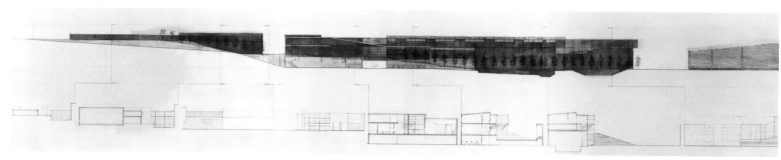

Alexandra Barker MArch '98, Analytical Sections, East Boston Site

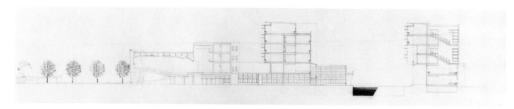

Section

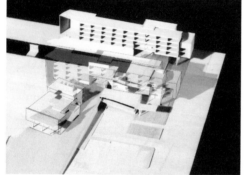

Markus Schaefer MArch '98, Model View

Suzanne Bowers MArch '98, Model View

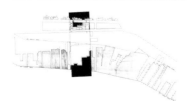

Mark Careaga MArch '98
East Boston Site Plan and Site Analysis

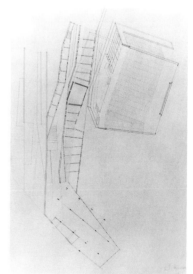

Wendy Weintraub MArch '98, Plan

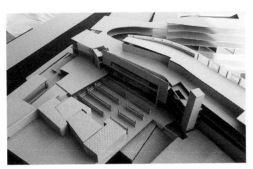

Karen Brandt MArch '98, Model View

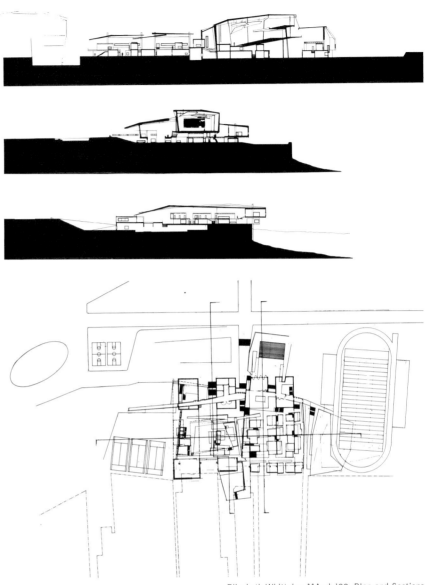

Elizabeth Whittaker MArch '98, Plan and Sections

Mimi Hoang MArch '98, Model Views

Lillian Smith MArch '98, Model View

Perspective View of Site

Site Study

Introduction to Landscape Architecture Design

Pierre David
MaryAnn Thompson, *coordinator*

Organized through three design projects, the studio introduced students to the basic concepts and means of structuring landscape architectural space. Each project explored issues central to the design of landscapes: the inherent complexity—conceptual and physical—of built landscapes and their relationship to historic, social, ecological, artistic, and geographic contexts; the interdependence between site and built form; and the temporal as an aesthetic dimension that is specific to the medium of landscape architecture.

The first project asked students to investigate a built landscape through a series of drawings that used the basic techniques of representation—plan, section, axonometric—as well as more speculative forms of representation and analysis, such as collage and bas relief. This introduced the students to the basic principles of composition, scale, ordering systems, as well as topography, orientation, and materials. The second project investigated issues of site. Starting with a study of the landform typologies of the New England landscape, students explored the basic operations involved in landform manipulation as well as the potential for design expression inherent in each type. Through an intensive series of daily exercises, using clay as the primary medium, students investigated issues of composition, texture, pattern, and scale as they pertain to the design of earthworks.

As a corollary to the landform workshop, students analyzed the physical and phenomenological aspects of three sites with different geological histories: a wetland, a drumlin, and an exposed bedrock site. Following the analyses, students added an element to one of the sites that described its physical structure and/or some aspect of its topology. The last project dealt with the redesign of the fragmented landscape captured within the system of overlapping ramps, driveways and crosswalks in the Fenway district of Back Bay Boston. The objective was to develop a strategy and program to engage the materiality of time and trans-formation, and their generative potential for design. Students were asked to interpret the richness of the site's phenomena without excluding the contingent aspect of sensual experience, occupation and re-creation. The challenge was to create a landscape that, escaping a pictorial or symbolic representation of the temporal, would be itself the medium/surface/ground upon which impermanence would be engaged or traced.

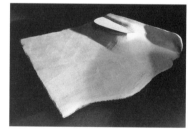

Christy Rogers MLA '98, Model View

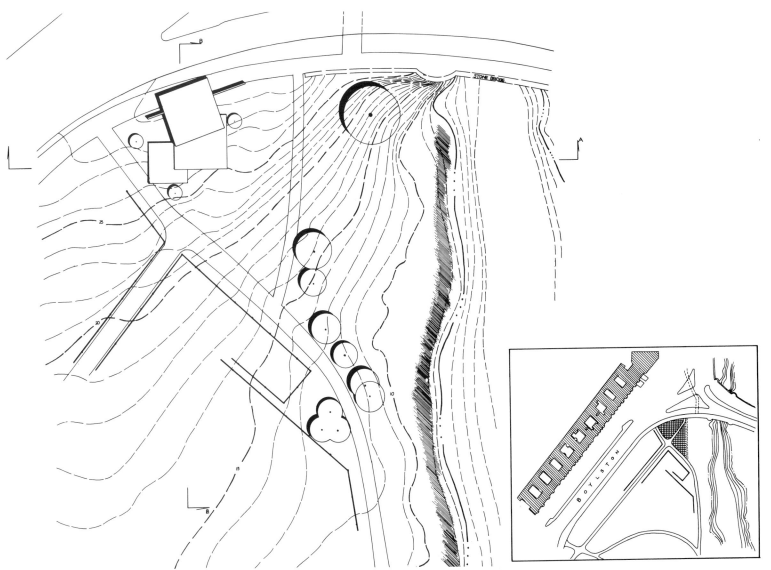

Tetsuya Fujie MLA '98, Plan and Context Plan: Victory Gardens Terrace, Back Bay Fens

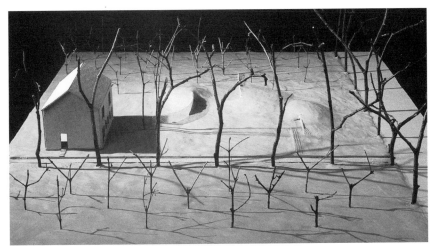

Cynthia Lordan MLA '98, Model View: Garden for an Avid Letter Writer

Section

Landscape Architecture Design

Gary Hilderbrand, *coordinator*
Paula Meijerink

This studio sought to extend students' knowledge and technique in the realms of program, structure, and site for domestic space. The semester began with analytical studies surrounding the program of the modern detached house. The second exercise involved a proposition for a non-site hideaway house for one. In this problem, the expressive possibilities of interior and exterior space were explored through enclosure, transparency, and overlap within narrow dimensional constraints. The project was then relocated to a small urban infill lot, where the issues of enlargement, orientation, adjacency, and a public face caused a transformation of the hideaway from the extraordinary/imaginary to the everyday/real.

The final iteration of the studio involved the confrontation of a dominant natural/cultural site condition. The project was once more transported to a one-acre parcel in a former rock mining quarry in a low-density area of Boston. Again, through transformation studies, students pursued the mechanical implications of massive rock and thin soil and the ecology of the urban regrowth forest as factors in shaping space for habitation.

Perspective Collage

Study Model

Chen-Kuang Chuang MLA '98, Site Plan

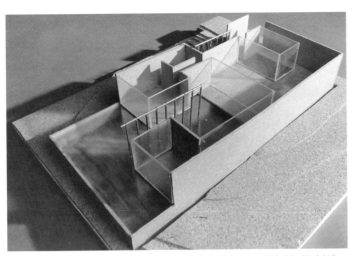

Christine Piwonka MLA '98, Model View

Sections and Elevations of Quarry Face

Katherine Bennett MLA '98
Model View of Quarry Site

Chad Adams MLA '97, Plan, Perspective, and Section of Park Proposal

Planning and Design of Landscapes

Niall Kirkwood, *coordinator*
Ken Smith

This studio reinforced and built upon the conventions of landscape architectural design production introduced in previous core studios and academic courses. Emphasis was placed on conceptual, schematic, design-development abilities, and on the elaboration of design strategies that may successfully address the interrelationship of context, site, and program. These skills were developed through a series of group and individual design studies located within the urban environment of Cambridge and Somerville.

Students inquired into the physical, socio-economic, technological, and ideological forces underlying the organization and form of human communities, and into the evolving concepts of urbanity, privacy, and commonality. The semester's work revolved around several key questions: What is the role of community design? Can a community result from the processes of design investigation and formal inquiry? Or simply put, can a community be designed? What are the key characteristics of urbanity? Can they be reinterpreted today and addressed through landscape architectural planning and design? In other words, can the design of human settlements and neighborhoods restore today the opportunity for choice, interaction, and that sense of belonging that traditionally characterized cities: If yes, how?

Three design problems, a mapping, an intervention of "additive transformation, and a landscape design proposal were undertaken in a study area stretching from the northern edge of the Harvard University Campus in Cambridge to the Boston and Maine Corporation Railway Tracks in Somerville.

For the first exercise, specific physical, technological, or socio-economic layers that make up the evolving settlement patterns of a number of cities were mapped. An analysis of the 'resonance' of these patterns and forces on a specific section or neighborhood of that city was carried out simultaneously with individual phenomenological and metaphorical interpretation of the study site. A specific program was provided for the second problem, a preliminary design intervention which tackled and promoted an "additive transformation" or infill on the site.
The final project involved development of a site program, and articulation of a specific site landscape design proposal.

Ruth Durant MLA '97, Plan: Park Proposal for Sears Site

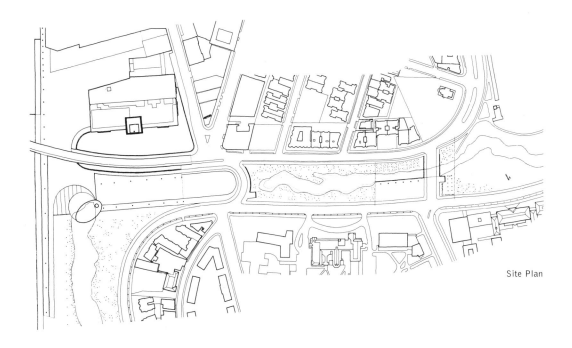

Site Plan

Raphael Justewicz MLA '97, Perspective View

Betsy Chaffin MLA '97, Model View

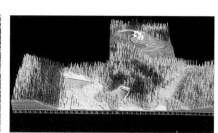

Raphael Justewicz MLA '97, Mary Muszynski MLA '97, and Julie Ruttenberg MLA '97, Model Views of Enso Community Site

Planning and Design of Landscapes

Douglas Olson
Carl Steinitz, *coordinator*
Rossana Vaccarino

Major objectives of this studio were to locate and design a large and intricate landscape and to develop abilities in organization, teamwork, and complex design decision-making, sometimes involving conflicting objectives (with particular emphasis on the relationship between social needs and landscape design at various scales).

Students explored issues of landscape planning and design, ranging from community-site location to detailed design of special places through a project for a new community for members of a religion (to be specified by the team), to be located in an historic New England town, Petersham, Massachusetts.

The problem statement given to students called for educational facilities, income-producing industry, residential accommodations for 100 visitors and 100 participants and their families, recreational facilities, and public facilities to accommodate up to 5,000 persons for special public events several times each year. Of concern to the existing town was the impact of a new community, especially on traffic, solid waste, water, and sewer infrastructures.

Working at diverse scales, three-person teams prepared a multiple-land-use site plan; individual students designed key elements within the overall scheme.

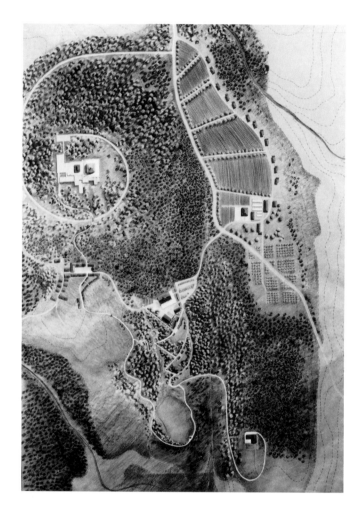

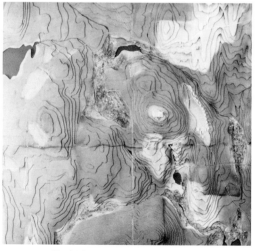

Chad Adams MLA '97, Ruth Durant MLA '97, and Edward Phillips MLA '97, Model View and Site Plan: Maitreya Community

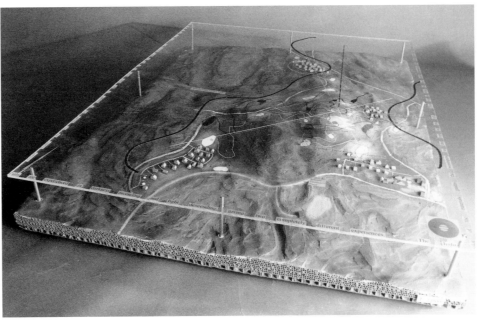

Scott Carman MLA '97, Betsy Chaffin MLA '97, Jane Choi MLA '97, and
Bertha Pantoja MLA '97, Model View of Esmoor Community Site

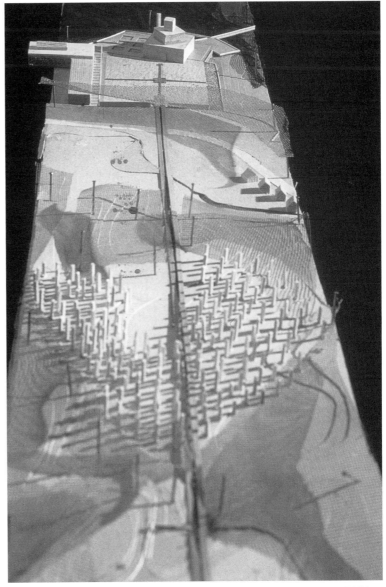

Cliff Garten MLA '97, Lisa Gramp MArch/MLA '97, Louise Wyman MLA '97,
Model Views of Wellspring Community Site and Sub-Basin

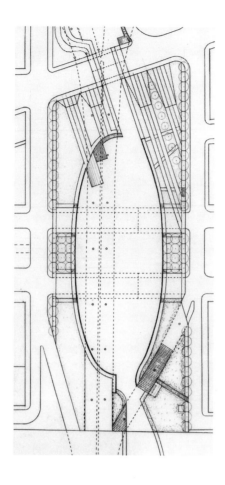

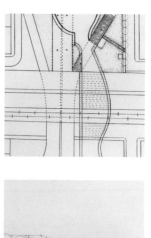
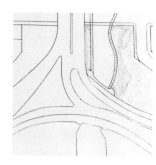

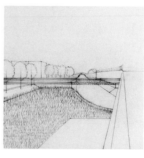
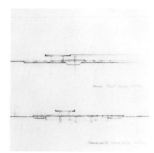

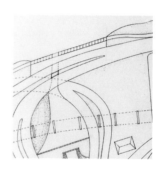
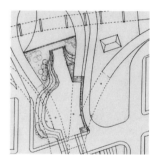

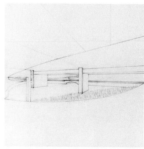
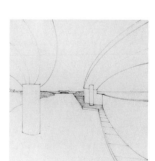

Landscape Architecture Design: MLA II Studio

Topographic Realms: Reforming the Back Bay

Gary Hilderbrand

The troubled intersection of the Back Bay Fens and the Charles River Basin is hidden under landfills, roadways, and a cloak of urban neglect. Far from its one-time status as the threshold and turning point for expansion of the city, it stands today as a stagnant littoral gap in the artificial land mass of the Back Bay. The site is riddled with bridges: pathway, highway flyover, railroad, boulevard, and abandoned street. The intention of the studio was to reconsider the conceptual and material conditions of bridging in the site, so that the confluence of these two significant urban drainageways could once again be reckoned as a defining force in the urban terrain. Beginning with the discrete intervention of a passage across the edge of the basin, the limits of the problem were then expanded slightly upstream toward a noble paradigm of urban connection, H.H. Richardson's Boylston Bridge. Here the students stared into the eyes of a bridge as landscape: no beginning, no ending, resistant to type, and piled up massively—almost amorphous, yet with proud and firm case. And in the shadows of this giant, the project sought to redefine the waterway as something to shape and something to be shaped by —a thing across and a thing to cross.

Tae-Wook Cha MLA '97, Plans and Perspective Views

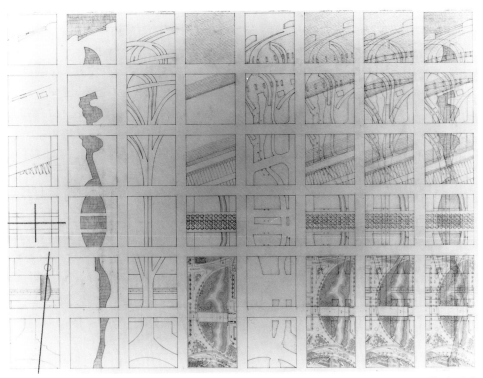

Site Analysis

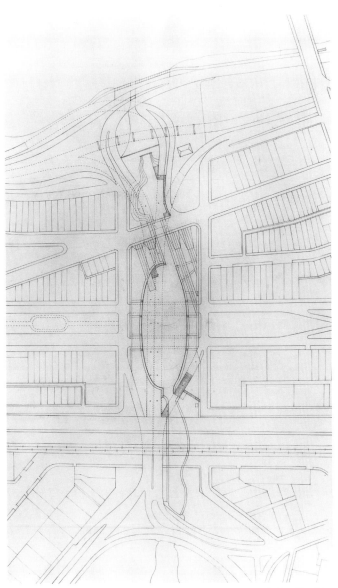

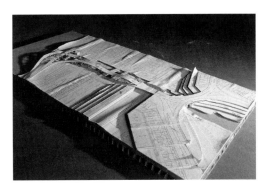

Model View

Tae-Wook Cha, Site Plan

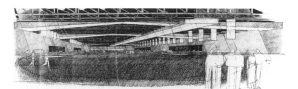

Perspective View

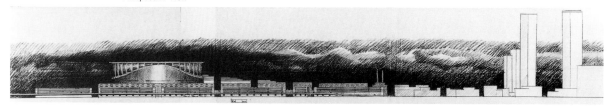

Elevation of Megaplex

Elements of Urban Design

Alex Krieger, *coordinator*
Rodolphe El-Khoury
Rodolfo Machado
David Neilson/François Vigier

This studio is one of two foundation courses for the Urban Design and Urban Planning degree programs. It emphasizes the development of a critical awareness of how the physical city affects and is affected by social, cultural, and economic factors. Conducted as both a studio and seminar/workshop, design problems tackle a number of issues: the interpretation of both traditional and contemporary paradigms for urban and suburban design; how urban concepts are represented; the interrelationship among streets, blocks, districts, parks, transportation corridors, and other components that make up contemporary urban environments; singular urban ideologies and their relationship to the history of urban design; as well as the implications of specific design strategies on the formulation of public policy.

Five related exercises introduced students to the basic elements of urban planning and design. The first design problem, an investigation of alternative configurations for Boston's City Hall Plaza and the surrounding area called Government Center, involved a consideration of essential characteristics of urban place-making.

The second exercise dealt with interventions and extensions to the city fabric by investigating the impact of a common historical catalyst for major urban change. Using nineteenth-century maps of European cities as a starting point, students prepared new city plans that responded to the introduction of a new form of transportation—the railroad—and its required network of infrastructure. The third exercise used a similar format to design a highway alignment on mid-century maps of several American cities.

The next exercise focused on housing and place-making in a suburban context. Beginning with an examination of contemporary definitions and perceptions of the suburb, students then tested the suitability and/or adaptability of more conventional urban patterns to a suburban condition by producing designs for a housing precinct based upon the research of a well-known prototype.

Finally, students developed re-use paradigms for urbanized districts whose original uses and purposes have, with modernization, become marginal or obsolete. Students focused on several Boston districts and on emerging long-range planning initiatives to recast their fortunes by promoting them as the backbone for the city's growing economic strength in the bioscience, medical research, and high technology industries. The aim of the exercise was a consideration of the role that urban design can play in the reinterpretation and/or economic resurgence of parts of the city that are presently assumed to be underutilized, undervalued, and in need of "reinvention."

Site Plan

Sean O'Malley MLAUD '97,
Diagrammatic Plan

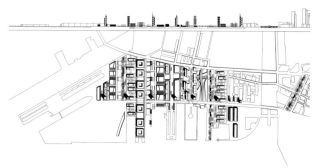

Site Plan and Section

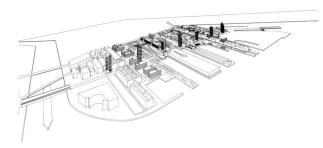

Thomas Rammin MAUD '97, Perspective View of Intervention

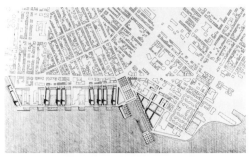

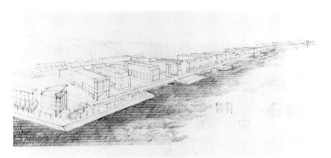

Site Plan

Diagram:
"Edges"

David Gamble MAUD '97, Perspective View

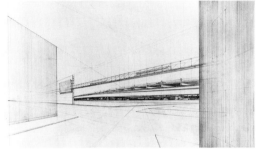

Model Views

Jeannie Meejin Yoon MAUD '97, Perspective View:
Big Box Retail Scape

BOULEVARD

SECONDARY STREETS

Master Plan

Plan Analysis

Alkistis Rodi MAUD '97, Site Plan

IMAGE: FRONT OF THE HIGHWAY

NEW HOTEL INDUSTRIEL SQUARE

Luis Bresciani MAUD '97,
Perspective Views

Theory and the Design Studio

In June 1996, *Studio Works 4*'s investigation of 'approaches' took the form of a discussion between several members of the GSD faculty exploring the relationship between theory and the design studio. Among other issues, the discussion considered whether theory can constitute an 'approach' in itself, the notion that theory might be pedagogically instrumentalized or implicit in a design studio, and the peculiar relationships to practice of both theory and design studio. Throughout, there was a struggle to define theory, especially to make a critical distinction between theory as it relates to the production of a design studio and Theory as a discipline in itself.

George Baird, Professor of Architecture (**GB**)

Preston Scott Cohen, Associate Professor of Architecture (**PSC**)

K. Michael Hays, Professor of Architectural Theory (**KMH**)

Linda Pollak, Assistant Professor of Architecture (**LP**)

Rossana Vaccarino, Assistant Professor of Landscape Architecture (**RV**)

moderated by *Studio Works* Student Editor, Jay Berman (**JB**).

JB A good way to begin this discussion may be the way Michael Hays begins his course on theory. Michael begins with two readings, Terry Eagleton's *Significance of Theory* and Edward Said's "Secular Criticism." Eagleton provides a fairly clear definition of theory. Each of you might begin by offering a definition of theory and then speculating about why we need theory.

KMH Eagleton says, and I guess I would adopt this for myself, that because we are human, because our existence is significant, in that we make signs in the practice of everyday life, we are theoretical. He refers to the fact that every time you let the cat out you are practicing some sort of theory at a rudimentary level. Because what we do is not governed by biology alone—one could say that architecture is not governed by just keeping warm and dry—we need theory to organize the sign systems we use. And Eagleton points out that theory is foregrounded in times when something has gone wrong. Theory is most

architectural theory is a particular pratice of transcoding. Theory, it seems to me, tries to discover or even invent the codes used by one kind of practice and transcode them into architecture to test what the result is.

—KMH

apparent when sign-making goes awry. Said stresses the situatedness of theory, asserting that theory is peculiar among academic disciplines in constantly reevaluating and historicizing itself and reevaluating its project, even its own terms. One way we might begin is to agree here on at least two distinctions. I think we can begin by agreeing that to make architecture is already to do theory. Architects produce concepts, they produce signs. And they've organized those signs and concepts. So making architecture is making theory. On the other hand, I guess that's not the same as analytical theory or critical theory, which takes the building as its object of study. If we think of criticism as evaluation of and commentary about the object, then I would say that theory is the discipline that tries to understand the terms, the concepts, the organization of criticism. And then there is meta-theory, which is the vocation of understanding theory itself. What will remain confusing for me is, how do we manage the distinction between architecture that produces theory and theory that produces architecture? Because that's what we're concerned with in the design studio.

LP   It's helpful to break it down into parts, and also to have up front Said and Eagleton, who are different in terms of the registers in which they define or understand theory. I would say that it isn't just that a theory changes in time, but that theory exists in many different theories at the same time, because there is the question of power in terms of which theories are on top.

KMH   I'd like to give another definition that I am operating with which is this: architectural theory is a particular practice of transcoding. Theory, it seems to me, tries to discover or even invent the codes used by one kind of practice and transcode them into architecture to test what the result is. That is to say, does it open up certain concepts that help us see architecture in a different way? But then alternatively, architecture also produces concepts. Architecture too is coded. And we can transcode the other way. I'm thinking of people like Frederic Jameson, Jacques Derrida, or even Michel Foucault who look to architecture because they find that transcoding from architecture into their own language helps them to articulate things that they couldn't otherwise. It again shows that architecture is already theoretical.

RV   How does this process of transcoding or inventing codes relate to studio? We are trying to separate these activities, possibly for the purpose of debate. I believe for you theory is not a deterministic vehicle meant to produce a specific design. It's not a preconceived overlay illustrated by an architectural product, nor is it an *a posteriori* justification floated over the object, right?

KMH   Right.

RV   Neither an *a priori* application of content, nor an *a posteriori* justification for what you might do would be an appropriate framework for operational strategies in studio. ... right?

KMH   I haven't gotten to the point that I can say what the exact role of theory is in the design studio. But maybe if we adopt this idea of transcoding, surely we can find examples of a student sitting at the desk who is somehow influenced or has in his mind certain feminist critiques, for example, that through some operation of transcoding would find a way onto the paper.

PSC The comment you made about Eagleton and signification going awry
is a key issue. I would say that all architectural practices are theoretical. But what if we were to take the particular case of a transgressive
project, or one that is critical as you say? When architectural design
becomes critical theory it involves, among other things, the transgression of codes of representation, codes that have to do with mediating
the relationship between the architectural spectator and the architectural object. Isn't that something in which the studio can immerse
itself—in the very processes that go into the conceptual underpinnings
of making? Isn't that where theory has to operate in studio, to go
directly to the problems of the medium that we employ?

KMH If you're foregrounding transgression, wouldn't we have to say that
that is one way that architecture has used theory historically, and
maybe we would even say that what you're calling a critical project
has been in recent history the one in which theory has been most
interested?

LP Meta-theory.

KMH No. Instrumentalized, transgressive theory. But, could we also say that
theoretical production in architecture could be about inventing new
codes, or elaborating old ones that aren't necessarily transgressive?

LP Or bringing together old codes in new constellations.

RV But, a number of studio critics present their design problems through
"problem statements" that are grounded in a particular ideological
framework. Those students who comply with that framework can initiate the design process sooner—because, in essence, the question and
the framework of the studio are not challenged. On the other hand,
students who resist the framework will have to expend additional
effort—effort that may not necessarily result in tangible production.
Unfortunately, professional standards often value physical production
over speculative criticism and theoretical discourse. I believe that studio should be a place for the production of knowledge rather than the
production of objects.

LP But one can reframe that process, so that through the production of
work in studio, a student is able to frame questions; the project isn't
set up to solve problems, but to frame questions.

JB There is a distinction to be made here. Scott and Michael are talking
about two very different projects. Michael is talking about one in
which the student sitting at his desk, passively adopts ideas that may
relate to the project. Scott is talking about the critical project, which
seems to be more actively engaged in what you might call theory with
a capital 'T' as opposed to theory in which all life is on some level
theoretical.

PSC I think that the studio framework is set up to anticipate that we
would aim to produce objects deserving acute critical attention. It
seems to me that the architecture that's produced here at the GSD
is not an architecture that is disinterested in critique.

RV How does this relate to the fact that many studio critics have a specific agenda that they want to present?

PSC That's an interesting question. I think they might come with the—
if you want to call it—agenda, that students would produce objects
more rarefied as far as theory is concerned, not part of everyday

practice as they see it in the profession. But within the core or options studios, the issue of representation is important. We immediately have to get involved in providing instruments to investigate and interrogate the inevitably inherited practices of architecture.

GB I have to say that I tend to be an ecumenicist in these kinds of discussions. Part of me wants to say 'all of the above.' Some of the time the relation of theory, design, and studio would be normative and relatively innocent: you might even characterize it as methodological. I'm thinking of the Eisenman studio for example, where the proposition is put forward that suggests that there are certain sets of techniques that are available and what's going to happen here is you're going to learn how they work. And the thing may be framed in a large context where the application of this method is in itself seen to be in some sense critical, broadly speaking. But the actual methodologies as they proceed in the studio proper are more or less how-to exercises. I don't have any problem with that as one of a set of available ways of proceeding, which forms a legitimate part of design praxis. And indeed I would have thought that when you characterize these procedures as ideological, I'm not sure that it doesn't amount, some of the time, to exploration of putatively exemplary procedures. As long as that's not the only thing happening, I think that's fine. Now that's not to say that one couldn't also have what I would characterize as a complementary mode that would be more theoretically self-conscious. And I guess in that sense one could call it meta-theoretical, which is critical at the scale of the methodology itself, or even a bit less aesthetic and more political. I wouldn't be inclined to privilege any of these in respect to each other, because it seems to me they all have a relative legitimacy as part of a constellation of approaches that is more or less theoretical.

Students have to be able to construct a position for themselves, and that could not leave out theory

—LP

LP There are different terms on which an artifact is conceptualized and made that don't necessarily have the capacity to 'see' each other. So you can say that students need to be able to acknowledge and move through some of these different ways of conceiving relationships between theory and practice because they need to establish their own ways of thinking as architects in each project that they do, and eventually in their thesis. Students have to be able to construct a position for themselves, and that could not leave out theory.

PSC That's an important point about positions—actually, in relation to practice. I don't think theory as a critical project puts its attention to architectural projects in design studios. The fact that the design studio has a hypothetical relationship to practice is not really part of the problem that theory reflects on with regard to practice. It's problematic to model a studio in relation to theory the same way practice might be modeled in relation to theory. Studio design brackets and puts more of its focus on the problems that can be managed in the atmosphere of the academic studio. It necessarily cuts off many issues that are of interest to critical theory.

KMH Like the political dimension, the economic dimension.

PSC In core, to a great extent, studio cannot involve direct negotiations with all of the parties and politics that would necessarily be involved in such projects.

GB You're making me a bit nervous. I don't dispute that academic studio projects are different from practice—but I would have thought that the primary way in which they were different is that the pedagogical projects are set up like gymnastic exercises to build particular muscles, deliberately excluding some parameters of a larger reality for the sake of placing the focus somewhere else. And so that's a pedagogical emphasis and it's a legitimate and necessary one.

PSC Yes.

GB But I wouldn't have been inclined to ascribe to that distinction a great theoretical status in itself.

LP Issues of the political and the social have to do with questions of representation. A studio is not altogether different from being involved in the schematic phase of a design project—certainly of a design competition, where the architect does write the parameters, basically. Because the artifact doesn't ever get to exist in the world, there's a kind of political dimension lacking in terms of the aspects of realism.

> *pedagogical projects are set up like gymnastic exercises to build particular muscles, deliberately excluding some parameters of a larger reality for the sake of placing the focus somewhere else.*
>
> **—GB**

PSC The question, then, is how does theory in the design studio help to distinguish those moments where political intervention is the main point as opposed to others that involve the codes of representation that the studio itself is immersed in?

KMH I will not be as ecumenical as George and stop me if I am. But I have a feeling that if we look historically, the whole idea of architect as cultural critic through form—architecture's avant-garde role or Scott's transgressive critical role—is very recent. In the 1980s, because of various economic reasons, building took off and architects became less reflective; that critical role of architecture got transferred to theory itself. The very idea of theory got associated with critical avant-garde transgression, and that has clouded our larger perception that theory is much more than just that. I think related to this is the problem that we became so successful at theorizing the critical condition of form—complex geometrical and syntactical relationships—that we actually theorized ourselves out of an ability to see how architecture exceeds form. Theory actually gave us a way of seeing one kind of thing—a complex, formal thing—so clearly, that it precluded us from seeing others. I think we're going to see a turn in theory. Some people call it a return to an interest in the body or tectonics. I think that those are both euphemisms for looking at what architecture does beyond strictly formal relationships. That too will be theoretical; this interest is a product of theory; it's just we haven't theorized it as well yet.

LP Maybe it's not as straightforward to theorize.

GB I agree with Michael about the narrowness of that particular focus, how it became self-reflexive, and the scope of theoretical praxis even began to get closed down a bit. Given that, why not explore some other modalities? It doesn't even say that those interests are illegitimate; it just suggests that they would benefit from some cross-fertilization.

KMH Now let me try this, though, so we can disagree. I think I would join with Scott in saying that theory would always have a vocation of looking for alternatives to what we have, and in that sense would be critical or forward-looking. And this is a political dimension. And maybe then, in some future, there would be some society so well-functioning that there would be no need for a theoretical alternative. The ultimate ambition of theory would be that it would not be needed. That is to say that we would have achieved the society that all of us through theory are trying to project. But let's face it, we're not there now.

LP But do you think theory solves problems?

GB I wouldn't put it so much in the context of a social politicization. Isn't there the process of designing and creating the expectation of some transcendence of known thresholds?

LP It isn't necessarily a transcendence of known thresholds but somehow an arrival at a threshold, and the possibility for transformation.

GB Yes.

JB I'm interested in Linda's question: does theory solve problems?

KMH There would be a normative kind that can solve problems. But I would say that theory, even a non-normative kind, produces the conceptual tools for solving problems.

LP Wouldn't that start to be kind of close to an architecture that defined itself as functionalist? In so much of architecture that's produced, significance can be obscured very easily by readings that are closer to the surface than other readings that are more difficult to theorize. So very often students are legitimating their work through how well it functions or how well it solves problems.

GB Certainly architecture doesn't solve any problems.

RV I think this goes with the issue of labeling design as either a problem-solving...

LP That would be one way of conceptualizing design—as something that solves problems.

KMH Wait—we don't want to do that.

LP Right. Deleuze and Guattari distinguish between the theorematic and the problematic as means of approach, saying that the theorematic, by dichotomizing theory and practice, doesn't work from within the work. With the problematic, on the other hand, the intellectual work happens through practice.

PSC That raises an interesting question about problematization. Jay said it: on one hand there's theory that constructs the problem or explains what should be done very explicitly. And on the other, there's theory that would be more implicit.

LP Or more reflexive.

PSC   What happens to the part of the architectural design project that exceeds the theory that somehow is instrumentally engaged?

LP   Why do you have to say instrumentally?

PSC   Well I was speaking before about the kind that is not instrumental, the kind of theoretical approach that only puts its attention to an interpretive framework that does not require forming the design in a specific manner. What happens to the part of the design that has not been required to be formed in relation to a particular theory? The reason why the first model is useful is because it requires us to interrogate all of those modes of interpretation of objects that we use in the medium, such as drawing, as opposed to those that are verbal. So I'm not clear—when we talk about theory floating above or not applying direct pressure to design—where does the rest of design go? Does it become just purely aesthetic excess?

GB   You might be meaning phenomenological or bodily considerations. On the other hand you might be meaning construction costs.

PSC   Uh oh.

GB   I'm not sure what the form of the exclusion is that you're making here.

LP   You might mean an architecture that purports to account for the way that the work looks through the logics of the work, when in fact the work requires decisions at all different points that have come from an unacknowledged aesthetic base.

PSC   Michael talked about the student at the drawing board cogitating upon questions of feminism and having them infiltrate his sensibility but not surface directly in the work. The question is, what about all the work that escapes from that?

RV   Are you trying to say that you want to find a place for theoretical inquiry in studio because it is important? Or because it's not really taking part in the design process as a catalyst?

theory helps address difficult concepts such as the 'public.' What is the 'public'? You reframe it with theoretical discussion in the studio before you even design a public space.

—RV

PSC   As theory takes less 'body,' more of the architecture escapes from it. And the question is, what to do about it? I'm talking about the aesthetic level in the studio. I'm talking about the muscles that theory is not exercising.

GB   But you see, that's one of the reasons for my ecumenicism. I would see that as a challenge to formulate other pedagogical models that speak to precisely the questions that are being excluded. And I see that as a kind of locus of pedagogical information. To go back to the muscle-training analogy, before the Olympics start you want this athlete to have trained all the muscles that are going to be needed. So it seems to me there's a pedagogical challenge there to invent techniques that cover some of these excluded considerations. And I like the idea of studios even being somewhat idiosyncratically formulated in order to achieve this result.

JB   It seems that you're all talking about using theory in a rather instrumentalized way.

KMH   Instrumentalized? Yes, I would agree with that.

sometimes we tend to confuse the kind of theory... which takes place from within the studio, with an analytic kind of theory, which goes by the same name, 'theory,' which tries to show that the thing produced had to be produced, that there weren't alternatives because a particular moment in history did not allow thinking in a different way.

—KMH

JB   And it seems to me that that would intersect in a peculiar way with students asking 'what is the relevance of theory?'

KMH   Let's come back to some distinctions. Because in some sense, I would still insist that theory does solve problems. Or, it doesn't solve problems, but it produces the concept of the solution. That's part of its relevance for studio, that it articulates the terms and categories out of which architectural strategies and techniques arise. But the relation of theory to design techniques is a highly mediated one; it's not direct.

RV   In my case, for landscape architecture, theory helps address difficult concepts such as the 'public.' What is the 'public'? You reframe it with theoretical discussion in the studio before you even design a public space.

KMH   The 'public' is a very helpful example. If we could theorize a public, and I'm not sure we have, wouldn't that then help us generate the techniques for a solution?

LP   My sense is that an architectural project is interesting at the moment when design and research are the same thing. A studio investigation about questions of publicness would require a narrower field in which those questions could be more productively investigated. The more limits that are placed on the project through or by the studio, the more likely it will be that the project isn't only an illustration, but can begin to look at the question in terms that actually acquire a certain physicality or spatiality, or engage issues of representation in ways that wouldn't be achieved otherwise.

RV   You reformulate a question at the start of the studio so that studio work might also be theoretical practice; the effort would not be to answer the question but actually to reframe the question.

LP   More precisely.

RV   And sometimes you don't have the answer.

KMH   I agree with the way you just formulated it: the goal may not be to find answers in that sense of solutions. But I do think theory has a social instrumentality, at least. Or that theory's instrumentality is social, in the sense that it tries to conceptualize a problem in order that it can be addressed. I think sometimes we tend to confuse the kind of theory that was just being described by Rossana and Linda, which takes place from within the studio, with an analytic kind of theory, which goes by the same name, 'theory,' which tries to show that the thing produced had to be produced, that there weren't alternatives because a particular moment in history did not allow thinking in a different way. That's a very different kind of theory that will always be, let's say, negative—which will always show why things had to happen, because at that moment humans could only think in this way because of certain ideological constraints.

LP   That's the 'theory as difficult history' model.

KMH   But I think what happens is, in courses at the school we tend to go back and forth between those two modes without always saying that we are doing so. And so theory, all of it, gets described as negational.

LP But many things go by the name of theory. I think one of the things you're talking about would be, say, post-colonial theory, now.

KMH Right.

LP Another would be—what I'm talking about—architecture dealing with space as structures of social relations. I think that this has to do with understanding the architect as bringing things from the world and projecting things into the world.

PSC Yes, but projecting into the world, the criticism implies the object.

LP Right.

PSC As opposed to the reflective.

LP Other ways might have to do with foregrounding the means of representation, not only in relation to a particular social question but in relation to its own possibilities.

PSC The same sort of division you made is also what I'm talking about between studio as a representation or simulation of practice, versus studio as an enterprise that speculates on architectural problems.

KMH When you said practice you mean office practice, right?

PSC Yes. Just now, I mean the production of buildings in the environment.

KMH Because when George and others use practice it means something very different.

GB I was using it in two ways. There is practice in studio itself, associated with practice as you just described it. But some of the time I was referring to practice in precisely the same way—the production of real buildings for construction in the real world.

LP In other words, the definition of practice is as difficult as the definition of theory. But if we are thinking about definitions we could go back to the question of method. Because how you make the artifact isn't really separable from what the artifact ends up being, but method is a way of getting between theory and practice.

RV Which means that perhaps the process of making, the method of the studio, could be critically 'open'; perhaps there should not be a prescriptive framework.

LP I'm talking about foregrounding the means of representation, so that one is aware that when one is making models at certain scales, for example, one is able to conceptualize the work and space in different ways than with models at other scales. If I tell my core studio that I want to work with sections at different scales and sectional models and perspectives, to have sectional thinking present in the studio throughout the semester as a way of countering a figure-ground approach to the city, that would be a studio-wide experiment. Maybe you wouldn't call that method but I would.

KMH We can call it method; we can call it technique.

LP But it could be a new way.

GB I would say within the territory of methodologically oriented studios, you could still have ones which were more directive.

LP   It just might be helpful to be able to use the terminology surrounding the methodological, to deal with a lot of what we're talking about. But the question of method is not separable from the question of basic skills. If you are teaching basic skills, how do you inflect it enough so that students get an awareness of how different skills privilege different ways of thinking?

GB   For me the whole thing is *a priori* situational. We are thrown into the world, and we've got to operate with the situation as found. I'm not against increasing the level of self-conscious awareness. But the idea that we're going to get to something that we can identify as basic and endorsing it, I think is both wrong and dangerous.

KMH   Because again, if you think historically, there would be a moment when the idea existed that painting buildings primary colors was a basic skill. There's also a moment when that's unthinkable, and it may actually be unthinkable now. And so, too, will there come a moment when —

PSC   Typology...

KMH   Yeah, that if typology was as basic to architecture as it has been, maybe it is now unthinkable. So these "basic skills" come and go rather quickly. But that's something to ponder.

GB   Before this thing finishes — this would involve the students — I think it's worth saying a little bit about instrumental and non-instrumentalized theory. Because I would hold the view that theory in studio is always instrumentalized. And you know, that's fine. It's informative and helpful that it be so. But at the same time I don't think theory in the curriculum is limited to instrumental theory, and so it does seem to me that another of the intellectual distinctions that is worth making is between the uses of theory in studio, which are obviously instrumental for just commonsense reasons.

LP   But why? Are all the uses of theory in architecture instrumental?

GB   Well, ultimately, I would say yes. Taking Mark Wigley's controversial remark at the theory symposium [at the GSD in the Fall of 1995], at the end of the day I think his claim is undeniable that theory's sole obligation is to say how things are.

KMH   Not to say how they —

PSC   Should be.

GB   Yeah.

LP   Then what is the thinking that you do to establish a way of thinking as an architect in order to make a particular project?

KMH   I still think it's helpful if we make distinctions between the city, the public, or the building, and the concepts of the city, the public, or the building. If we make that distinction and say that theory deals with concepts, then it seems to me that this problem of instrumentality and of negotiating analytic theory or critical theory with applied theory goes away — in fact, this whole discussion of instrumentality goes nowhere, it seems. Take Linda's example of post-colonialism, which tries to explain a certain historically specific event by producing a

> *if...theory deals with concepts, then it seems to me that this problem of instrumentality and negotiating analytic theory or critical theory with applied theory goes away*
> —KMH

I believe that studio should be a place for the production of knowledge rather than the production of objects.

—RV

concept of those events. It also begins to show you a way that you can devise techniques to make buildings or cities that redress situations or that organize the situations. I'm not saying that's an easy or direct process. But it is a process of implementation.

PSC Is that something you'd like to see a studio pick up?

KMH This is the first time I've actually focused on this, but because George makes the distinction so radical, you start looking at negotiating that space in-between. And I think that space is negotiable. Because once you have concepts then you can start generating techniques.

JB That's not instrumental?

KMH Well, I think it makes the issue of instrumentality a non-issue. Of course it's instrumental at some level at some times.

RV It becomes an inevitable response to it.

KMH Exactly.

LP Maybe I still don't understand, but does instrumental mean that you're using something to do something?

KMH The pejorative version of instrumentality would be where the status of the use exhausts the phenomenon.

LP Because then I think there is a third way that is neither instrumental nor pure, where you posit something and you make a provisional position.

KMH Right.

LP And then it could come out in some very small piece of the project.

GB What you are saying is that it's within our nature to react, rather than for theory to describe the reaction.

RV And I think that happens already, inevitably between seminars and studio independently, even if they're not meant to be together.

GB What you've said is precisely Wigley's argument, theory in the morning and studio in the afternoon [with no necessary relation between them].

RV On the other hand, if you plan studio around a specific theoretical framework then it's somewhat prescriptive and deterministic; you have the instructor who invites particular guests, and then already you bias the studio.

GB That could be called instrumental.

LP Isn't it cynical, though, this theory in the morning, studio in the afternoon?

GB Theory in the morning means that the thing is presented in terms of its revelatory power. And what its implications are for architecture is left for a kind of seeping around the corners of the psyche.

KMH Method.

GB Method, that's right.

KMH And now if it plays itself out, in a secondary or tertiary way, it's all fine. But its status is not considered utilitarian.

PSC But then is a studio largely left to quote its own devices? Other than being seeped into by theory, what else is the studio doing?

KMH I'm not arguing that that's the only modality, Scott. I'm just saying that I don't have any problem with theory up to a point being instrumentalized in the studio. And that's why I'm saying I endorse these didactic methodological studios, which are very instrumental.

PSC Okay, but for the people who advocate Wigley's position [theory in the morning and studio in the afternoon], can you speculate for me what, if theory infiltrates one's sensibility, the project of the studio would be? What is the enterprise of the studio driven by? Is it driven primarily by these unconscious infiltrations?

LP That's really important.

PSC How does that model function? I'm not talking about other models, I'm talking about that model.

KMH You've just presented that that model is obviously flawed in a big way.

PSC But it's a big model.

KMH I don't think it's a big model.

PSC I do.

KMH I like the way Rossana put it. The response, the reaction, is inevitable. If someone theorizes something, somebody else is going to respond.

RV And there is a next question I ask myself. In the curriculum, it's important that studio occurs within cross-disciplinary discourse. On the one hand, seminars should be conceived in their possible application to studios. They are independent, in a democratic way, but they also overlap. On the other hand, there are situations where in studio there is this resistance to this healthy reflection. And so it's impossible to get theory in.

KMH They want to keep studio pure.

LP But that's the basic skills ideology.

> *But isn't it also true, though, that the same way that putting out the cat at the end of the day is theoretical, there ain't no studio being taught that is also not theoretical?*
>
> —GB

GB But isn't it also true, though, that the same way that putting out the cat at the end of the day is theoretical, there ain't no studio being taught that is also not theoretical?

PSC Yes.

GB It's just a question of how explicit or implicit it is.

PSC But for example, when we speculate that typology might become unthinkable as the primary focus of design, and when other very specific devices that produce architecture just dissolve, and other techniques of representation start to become difficult to grasp in a direct manner, I'm sorry, but that is the moment when the Wigley model becomes the dominant model. In this situation, studio doesn't have its own body of knowledge and techniques that are clear. I'm talking about a general condition that I think we're facing more and more.

KMH But you're asking us to imagine architecture—

PSC It's already happened—

KMH Without theory, and I think—

LP Architecture as illustration.

PSC No, I'm talking about a moment when it becomes less possible to be specific about the production of the artifact, to account for its particular—

LP When you say we, you don't mean you?

PSC I'm speaking generally about architectural culture.

LP A breakdown of older paradigms.

PSC That's right.

GB For me there's a pedagogical condition that qualifies your anxiety somewhat, and that is the fact that most of the characterizations of the relationship of theory to designing that we have formulated so far tend to have the characteristic, to some degree, of being didactically exemplary, and that designing follows from them. But, of course, we all know perfectly well that one equally powerful modality of theorizing is demystification, where I think that precedent is so pedagogically important. The object of study already exists and is provisionally taken on its own terms. And of course, in the beginning we don't even know what 'taken on its own terms' means because it's in the process of being defined by the procedures. Then, the power of theory is in the kind of discoveries of hitherto unforeseen characteristics of that artifact.

PSC Yes, and that's what Michael is talking about.

GB And that's easily as powerful a mode of theorizing as saying 'these are the rules, now go and draw it up.'

PSC This is what I would like to hope—that you can propose ways of making and working within codes that are not meta-theorized in advance.

> *Increasingly, I think, even among students, there's a kind of bottom-line sensibility that theory is a luxury that we can't afford: just tell us what to do and let's get on with it.*
>
> **—KMH**

KMH Good. I think among those sitting in this room there's obviously a respect for the issue and a desire to wrestle through the question you put to us. But we have to remember that there is presently a theoretical backlash. Increasingly I think, even among students, there's a kind of bottom-line sensibility that theory is a luxury that we can't afford: just tell us what to do and let's get on with it. That's prevalent among students and in the profession. That's very peculiar for architects. Architects have always been completely immersed in their intellectual culture, and the idea that architects should not read Foucault, Barthes, and Deleuze—if that's what theory means—is a very peculiar historical position. Architects have always been intellectuals, until recently. There is also the sense that theory is somehow just not needed. The idea that you can make an architecture without theory is so unthinkable to me, to have very prominent professionals saying that we don't need theory is actually dangerous. It's anti-intellectual. And I know it's because as theory was institutionalized, that kind of backlash was inevitable. And as it became too specialized it was inevitable. But actually, if we really think seriously about the issue, the anti-theoretical stances that are being taken now will look quite stupid historically.

LP   Even an issue as simple and straightforward as the precision or economy of a work are issues that are fed and supported through theory.

KMH I have a quote from Lenin. Not John, the other one. I can't recount it verbatim, but it's a lament that at this moment in time we have to make do with theory, the idea being that what we really want to do is precisely to instrumentalize it, to put it into practice. And at certain moments theory is just making do until you assimilate it and internalize it, so that then you can get on with the real work.

LP   That it becomes reality, so that they're not dichotomized.

KMH They're in no way dichotomized. Maybe we're in a period where we're making do with theory.

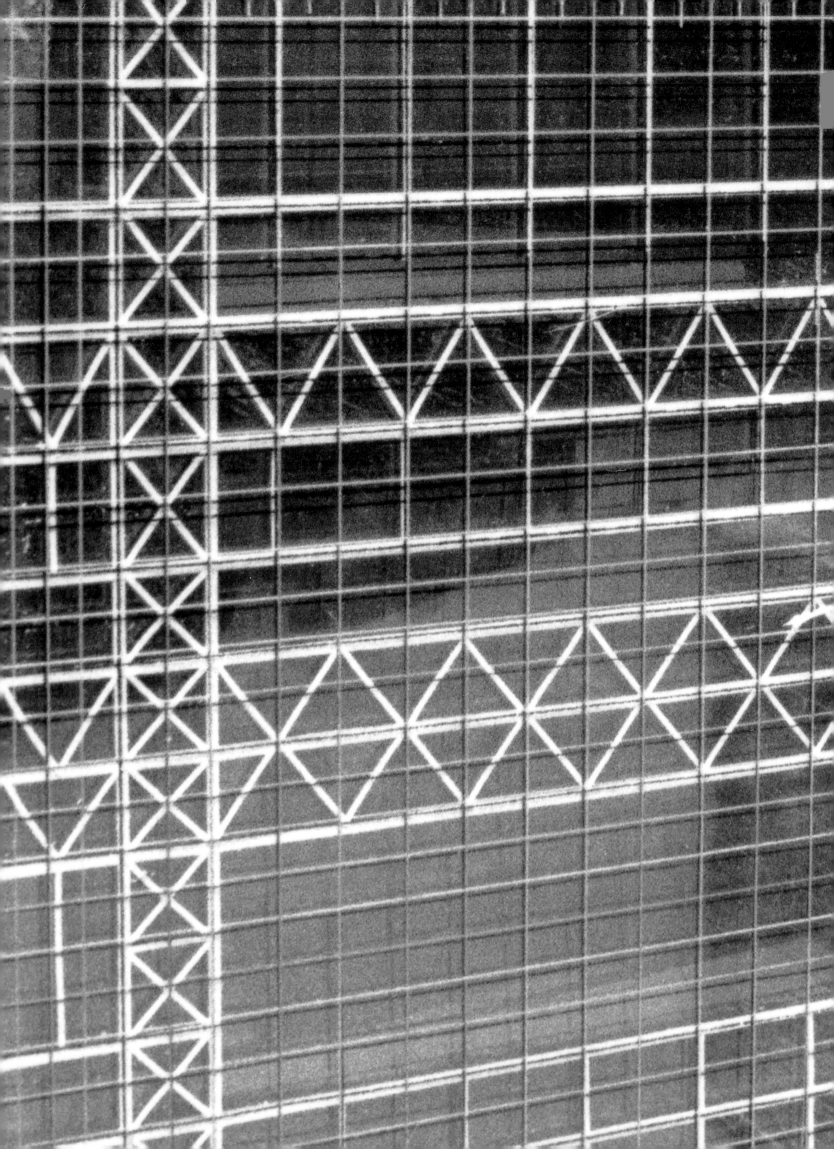

STUDIO OPTIONS FALL 1995

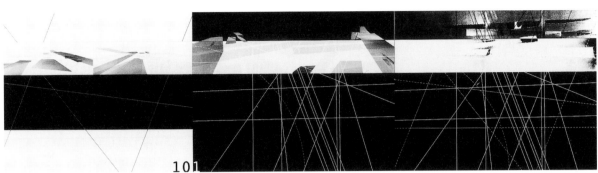

Chien-Ho Hsu MArch '97, Conceptual Site Drawing

The Architecturalization of Infrastructures

Marc Angélil and Sarah Graham
Visiting Critics in Architecture

Two realms of investigation were juxtaposed against one another within the studio work. The first pertained to the formation of contemporary urban developments for which the city of Los Angeles functioned as a case study.

The second involved the role of methodology within the design process. These two objectives were studied with a view to the potential of their mutual interaction.

Also addressed was the role of architecture within nontraditional large urban agglomerations for which Los Angeles could be considered prototypical. Los Angeles operates with a decentralized form of organization marked by expansion rather than by density. The urban fabric can be read as an overlay of various networks that form the infrastructural framework of the city. These structures do not pertain to unifying systems but instead manifest conditions of dispersal, discontinuity, and rupture. The way in which architecture is conceived within such an urban condition implies the potential of alternative strategies of formal invention and intervention.

Within this approach, traditional methodologies of design need to be reexamined. The methods of design production, specifically the relationship between content and process, can be redefined. This requires an exploration of the underlying structures as well as the means of the design process. Consequently, the design processes were at the core of the project. In this sense, the design studio was considered a laboratory, research constituting the modus operandi of the work.

In order to limit the scope of investigation, the architecturalization of infrastructure was tested as the programmatic hypothesis of the studio.

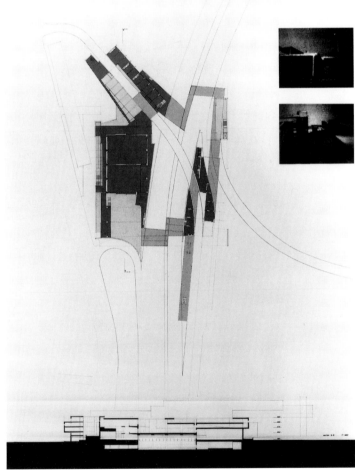

Thomas Juul-Hansen MArch '97, Plan, Section, and Perspective Views

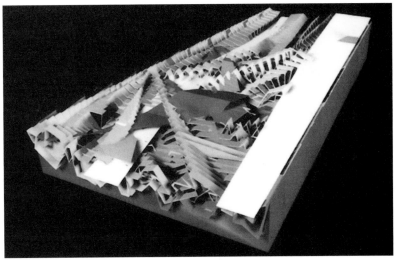

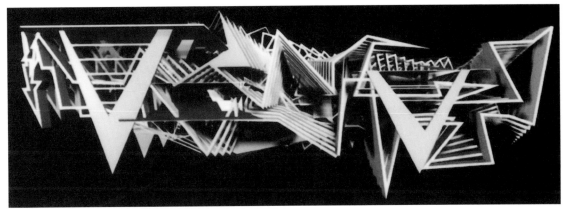

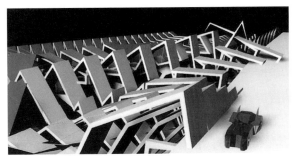

Perspective Views

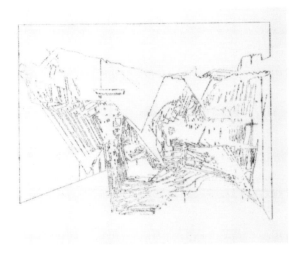
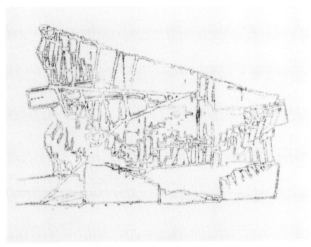

Shana Priwer MArch '97, Sections

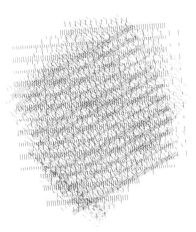

Spatial/Formal Studies

Haupstadt Berlin Stadtmitte Spreeinsel— The Spreeinsel Competition

Alan Balfour
Visiting Critic in Architecture

Berlin has been the focus of the world's architectural activity for the past five years. With the collapse of the wall, the idea of a united Berlin captured all imaginations—it could be reformed to become the most progressive city in the new millennium. The shape of this new city is beginning to emerge, created out of a series of competitions that have tapped the desires of architects around the world. No city in the twentieth century has provided such a revealing section through the aspirations of these times.

The last and most significant of these competitions was based on the redevelopment of the historic heart of Berlin, Spreeinsel, the island on the Spree that was the site of the most dominant structure in the pre-war city—the King's Palace, or Stadtschloss, the last Berlin home of the Kaiser. Its vast paternalistic presence was surrounded on the north by the cathedral and the heroic assembly of national museums, held in place by Schinkel's majestic Altes Museum and to the south by offices of government. The Stadtschloss was demolished by the government of the German Democratic Republic for political reasons—removing from the city the most powerful symbol of Prussian autocracy. On its site was constructed the symbolic center of the socialist regime, the Palace of the Republic.

The competition presented three problems. At its simplest it was a task of civic design and civic architecture, reestablishing a sense of place in the ancient heart of the city. In metaphysical terms it presented a struggle between conflicting desires whether to create a transformative progressive reality or reestablish historic order to the heart of the city, and it revealed a deep political conflict between those who wished to preserve the structures of socialism and those who wished to destroy them, and in so doing, weaken the social aspirations still so strongly present in East Berlin. The last two issues remain unresolved. Even before the competition was held, the first public construction in East Berlin after the wall was removed was to recreate in canvas the vast facade of the King's Palace.

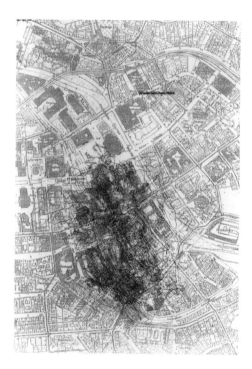

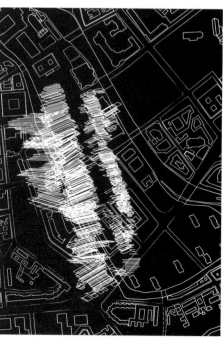

Robert Burrow MArch '96, Augmentation

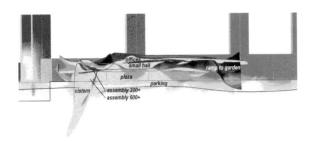

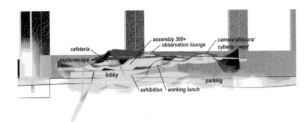

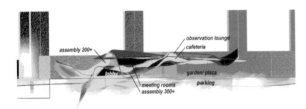

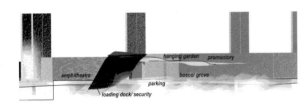

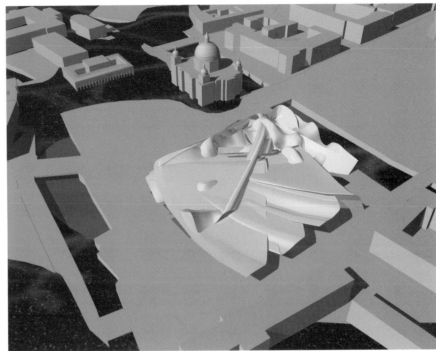

Aerial View of Conference Center, Altes Museum, and Cathedral

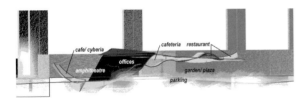

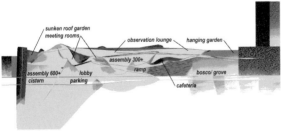

Wade Stevens MArch '97, Sections Through Conference Center

Gabriele Evangelisti, MIT, Model View

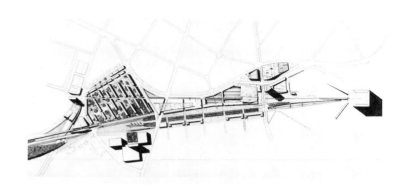

Master Plan

Western Extension of the Grand Axe of Paris

Jean-Pierre Buffi
Visitng Critic in Urban Planning and Design

Julia Trilling
Assistant Professor of Urban Planning

The site and scope of this project are exceptional: the wesern extension of the Grand Axe of Paris beyond the Arche de la Défense through Nanterre. The question posed was how to continue the city of Paris's historical axis by the creation of forms, spaces, and structures, etc., that will give a new urban image to the suburb of Nanterre, enhance the historic and symbolic significance of the Paris axis with a modern figuration, and employ the Axe as a "backbone" to rehabilitate the existing urban fabric. The project concerned that section of the axis where it will be necessary to restitch the two site sections of Nanterre now separated by an empty space—the university and low-cost housing development on one side and the Nanterre government and cultural center on the other.

Working in multidisciplinary teams the student project was to provide a response to three objectives: (1) design and plan the functional and spatial integration of the university and the city; (2) give form and identity to the public spaces; and (3) define an urban design and planning response that imposes a dual identity: that of a space belonging both to Paris and Nanterre.

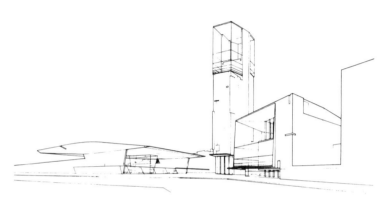

Perspective View

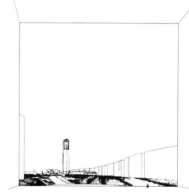

Adam Glazer MAUD '96, Perspective View Through the Arche de la Défense

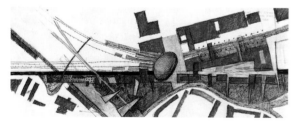

Interventions

Marcella Cortina Rodriguez MAUD '96 and
Maria Saidee Springall MArch '96, Analysis Drawings

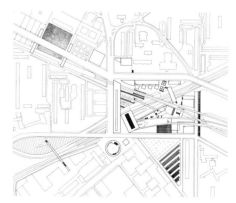

Jun Takahashi MAUD '96, Site Plan

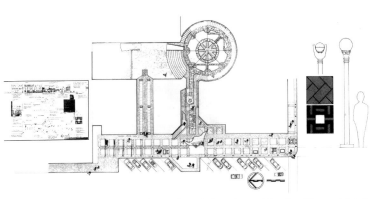

The Academy: Indiana Avenue Elevation, Plan, and Details

Derrick L. Woody MAUD '96, Master Plan:
35th Street and Neighborhood

Bronzeville I

Leland D. Cott
*Visiting Critic in Urban
Planning and Design*

This studio concentrated on the Grand Boulevard District of Chicago's South Side. This district forms the nucleus of one of the oldest and largest Black communities in the United States. As African-Americans began to migrate to Chicago during World Wars I and II, they were segregated into this neighborhood, which became known as Bronzeville. This virtually self-sufficient area, which had previously furnished jobs, homes, and social services to its residents, has undergone physical deterioration along with severe demographic, social, and economic change. Today Bronzeville is struggling to regain its character and vitality. As the neighborhood proceeds to experience modes of reinvestment, this studio aimed to assist in considering the role effective planning and innovative design thinking can play in successful community renewal.

During the first half of the semester, students worked on developing a comprehensive understanding of the neighborhood with an emphasis on the 35th Street corridor between Lake Michigan to the east and Comisky Park to the west. The identification of urban renewal strategies and the development of urban design and architectural guidelines for 35th Street were stressed. During the second half of the semester, work concentrated on the design of specific retail, institutional, and housing sites along the 35th Street corridor. With these uses as its principal focus, this studio promoted a dialogue between concerns for urban design, architectural design, and landscape architecture.

This studio was conducted in collaboration with the College of Architecture at the Illinois Institute of Technology. IIT and GSD students worked simultaneously on similar studio projects and jointly participated in neighborhood meetings, workshops, and presentations.

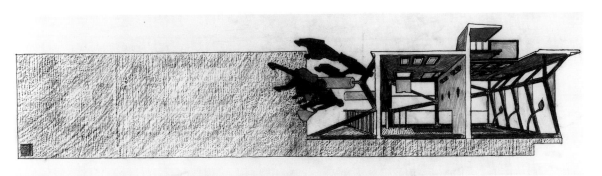

Perspectives of Proposed Gateway to Bronzeville Inspired by the Jacob Lawrence Migration Series

Nathaniel Fuster-Felix MAUD '96, Section/Perspective of Proposed Galleria

Thoughts on the Question of Approach

Any large-scale urban design undertaking calls for effective collaboration between urban designers, planners, architects, and landscape architects. In order to simulate an actual urban design and planning endeavor, I decided to organize these studios around student teams. To my surprise, every student team in Bronzeville I (fall semester) and II (spring semester) commented on the extra effort that was required to work cooperatively. Nonetheless, at the end of each semester, students seemed to agree that learning to work together was beneficial and that, in most cases, the quality of the product was enhanced by the team effort.

The Bronzeville I group was divided into two student teams of equal size. The first team focused on the historical significance of the surrounding African-American community as the organizing force for a community-wide master plan. The second team concentrated on the redevelopment of 35th Street, in the process creating a series of neighborhood "building sculptures" that incorporated the paintings of African-American artist Jacob Lawrence. The Bronzeville II studio was made up of four student teams of varying sizes. One team was organized around sustainable economic development, another around family empowerment and educational opportunity. A third team made the effort to create a series of urban gardens for the residents of a proposed low-rise housing community. The fourth and largest team proposed a dense urban development centered around the construction of a community-based renewable waste energy facility.

My pedagogical approach to teaching these studios emphasized three elements: first, immersion of the students in an inner-city neighborhood; second, encouragement of the use of interdisciplinary resources to understand the scope of problems of the neighborhood and thus to posit a range of design solutions; third, an insistence that all building types, but especially housing, are not isolated building forms but must be developed in the larger context of the neighborhood.

We visited our Chicago sites on five separate occasions—ultimately meeting with and discussing our work with scores of community residents. With neighborhood renewal being the core objective of the studios, I envisioned that this level of immersion would enable the students to expand their understanding of the role that innovative planning and design can play in revitalizing an urban community. As is the case with problem-solving in any discipline, defining the problem is the first order of business. An early lesson learned in both studios was that it is nearly impossible when working in an inner-city context to achieve consensus on problem definition. The multitude of stakeholders—residents, merchants, or whoever—frequently believe that another's gain invariably comes at their expense.

The scope of the studio problem meant that there were many possible approaches the designer could take in trying to address such inner-city problems as physical deterioration of buildings, overcrowding, family disorganization, and poverty. Early discussions in Bronzeville I and II focused on whether design was an appropriate response at all. Many students believed the problems in such an inner-city neighborhood were too severe and theorized that physical design would have little, if any, impact on the situation. Other students pondered what kind of design solutions could make a difference. Perhaps it is no wonder that even architects, planners, and urban designers questioned whether design could play a role in the improvement of the urban environment when faced with the worst urban ghetto in America! It was interesting, challenging and, of course, frustrating for students to attempt to design solutions to problems that for decades have resisted being solved.

Nathaniel Fuster-Felix, Perspective View of Proposed Galleria and Urban Space

Having had similar qualms about the role of design in the face of extreme poverty and hardship, I have, from time to time, in my own work relied on outside experts to help broaden the definition of the problem and therefore the possible solutions. Consequently, I decided to supplement the Bronzeville II studio with a series of evening seminars intended to explore a variety of related topics, such as public housing history and policy, the role of government involvement in the construction and management of public housing, and the importance of public health to inner-city renewal. In one instance, for example, we considered whether one can discuss the problem of inner-city housing without confronting the social inequalities of public health delivery in urban neighborhoods. My students were startled to hear one guest seminar leader—Dr. Lisa Berkman, Professor of Health, Social Behavior and Epidemiology at the Harvard University School of Public Health—state emphatically that what we do as the designers of the urban environment will have a greater influence on the health and well-being of inner-city residents than she will in her role as a public health provider! The semester was filled with these sorts of revelations, which served to broaden the design approach. We also integrated material from the Initiative for a Competitive Inner-City (ICIC) developed by Professor Michael Porter at the Harvard Business School. In my future Bronzeville studios, and beyond, I intend to call on other Harvard graduate schools to participate with us at the GSD so that we may share our perspectives on issues that architects have traditionally viewed as being primarily design-related. I believe the urban designer has the responsibility to facilitate just such an interdisciplinary approach.

In my role as design critic, I attempt to have my students see the interrelationships between particular building types and the broader context. I believe, for example, that the solution to the problem of housing and housing design must go beyond traditional and established parameters, which are too often limited to the design of physical form. My pedagogical objective is to teach that the design of housing is about people, neighborhoods, economic opportunity, educational possibilities, health-related issues, and so on. For me, this is the way to create physical form, spatial relationships, building mass, streetscape, etc. My own housing designs, for example, are most successful when elements usually seen as being outside the realm of the designer are brought to bear on the problem and, in fact, inform the eventual completed design. I think this can be very liberating and ultimately a necessary part of successful urban design and planning.

Leland Cott, FAIA, *is an architect and urban designer whose practice is based in Cambridge, MA.*
He currently holds an adjunct appointment at the GSD as Design Critic in Urban Planning and Design.

Pigeon Cove: Site Perspective

Edith Drcar MLA '96, Site Intervention

Mark Daley MLA '96, Water Study

Reaching for the Landscape

Pierre David
*Visiting Critic in
Landscape Architecture*

"…où pourtant aussi la solitude fait rage par une de ces fantasies de la nature qui, autour des cratères de l'Alaska, veut que la neige demeure sous la cendre…"

L'amour fou. André Breton, 1937

[*"…this is also where solitude rages by one of these fantasies of nature where, around the craters of Alaska, snow remains beneath the ash…"*]

Ia. Landscape never begins, it is always too late.

Ib. We studied two sites simultaneously. The first site was real and the second was imaginary. The first site consisted of a three-mile stretch of coast, reaching half-a-mile inland and half-a-mile out to sea. The second site was a mental landscape that was necessary in order to study the first.

IIa. Students had to invent ways to enter the landscape in different places. The landscape could not be entered where it begins, but rather where it slows down between legends and objects.

IIb. For both sites students were asked to make maps, each with a legend. These maps showed different processes. They were then superimposed to obtain different kinds of readings. This "layered" landscape hints already at things to come. Following this the studio discussed a "necessary program."

IIIa. Transporting our body together with our soul into the heart of landscapes, the studio discovered, all of a sudden, remarkable spaces. These spaces were "over-determined" in comparison to the patient state of expectancy in which we find ourselves.

IIIb. This third moment consisted of transferring the power of the images belonging to the mental landscape into the real landscape. Students' designs took place at the point where both realms meet.

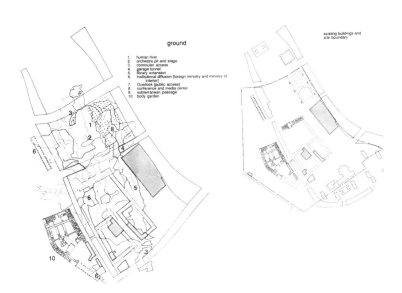

Keith O'Connor MLAUD '96, Site Analysis: Rips and Tears in Corrugated Metal
Siding, Broken Windows, and Translucent Plastic Panels

To Work Within the Condition of a Society

In the end, it is not enough merely to understand what we are doing to our planet, as if we were observing the changes through a giant telescope on Mars. Because we are all members of a world citizenry, we also need to equip ourselves with a system of ethics, a sense of fairness, and a sense of proportion as we consider the various ways in which, collectively or individually, we can better prepare for the twenty-first century.

Paul Kennedy, *Preparing for the Twenty-first Century*, 1993

To work within the condition of a society

Fisherman

Experts at the Habitat II Congress in Istanbul attested to the population explosion in the Third World. In 2015 Third World cities will be home to more than half the world's population. Cities in the industrialized world do not come close to approaching the same rate of population growth. Estimated population growth by 2015 in Paris is 2%; in Dacca 157%. The Industrial Revolution transformed cities into tools of production—the foundations of a city were determined by the richness of its soil or its geographic location.

Today the shape of cities is changing because the conditions of production in our society have changed. New technology allows us to work away from the city: we no longer need to visit the urban center for information exchange or to buy and sell goods. But will we be able to live spread-out from one another and still maintain the social ties that gave birth to cities?

To Progress

A city no longer needs to grow adjacent to another city for progress to take place within the landscape. The new pattern leaves space between old limits and new points of development, creating places geographically remote from one another, connected by a multitude of networks.

Our work as architects and landscape architects is to locate and equip these new loci: at the bend of a river, or between two highways. We must insist that we believe in the resources of each of these locations ourselves. Each place is linked to the others. Those with identical strata will reveal continuity; those with different strata will reveal discontinuity.

Just as archeologists, we must study layer after layer of the landscape. We can look at the anthropological, geographical, and ecological aspects of these places to better understand the common links between them. We should be able to find in each locus what gives it its identity. A natural geographical condition—the path in which a river flows—needs to be understood as a link between the places it passes. An artificial situation—the embankment of a highway—should be considered as relevant as one of the Seven Hills of Rome. The goal of our work is to assure that each place is known for its identity.

Stones

We need to consider that each place possesses its own conditions of spatial and programmatic modification. Therefore, a park must act as an expression of the conditions of the place and its foundations. Because these places are evident but their boundaries are less clearly defined, the park is an interval of the world.

Places persist even where a common thing—a dynamic resource—does not emerge due to a lack of differentiated space or because of confusion that makes it difficult to study the historical strata of a place. Nevertheless, when a city is built where natural resources are nonexistent, we must invent spatial condensers. The garden can substitute for the heterogeneity of the landscape. The garden becomes the world—a condenser, a laboratory, a tool with which to weave the social fabric. In other words, a garden can represent the explanation in the parentheses that gives a text deeper meaning.

At times architecture has the power to turn space onto itself, creating a garden while simultaneously, through phenomenal transparency, creating a park.

OMA/Rem Koolhaas, A House in
the Netherlands, 1992-1993

To see this subterranean thing

It is almost how I look at the map of a landscape I do not know—the map of long lines, long horizons of the coast, stretched lines, vagabond lines around the rocks. It is almost as, early in the morning, I look at the rings under the eyes of the woman I love, lines darker than the transparent skin of the face, containing memories of past times. Do they suggest the fragility of the body, a true transparency, or a possible access to the soul? What if this geography of the face were the sign of passage and recollection all at once? Wouldn't it be from there that desire arises? Desire digs at the surface of the country as well; there are always rings, places to access the landscape.

Mark Rothko, *Untitled,* 1954. Yale University Art Gallery

In the landscape, permanence and mutation exist together, as if what we observe is only the last ripple in the water after we throw in a rock. A vivid emotion embraces us at the top of a hill, during the summer, north of Forqualquier. The vision of a white, horizontal line lifted from the ground, a line in suspension seizes us; it is the line of the vague landscape of Provence suddenly becoming the sharp spurs of the Alps. Is it this suddenly shrinking space that creates the wind that André Breton called *"une aigrette de vent aux tempes"*? A meaning uncovered by the unconscious abruptly crosses our bodies to appear, through successive shivers, at the contact of our skin with a mysterious other. We inhabit the subterranean thing.

Isn't there in the etymology of the word subtle the idea of a hidden meaning, sub tela, under the canvas? What would be subtle would be the itinerary to discover this clandestine thing. I think about Italian frescoes—about Piero della Francesca in Arezzo, Giotto in Assisi, Fra Angelico in San Marco: painters who give me instant pleasure. In the making of frescoes, meaning cannot lie between the colored and the canvas; the wall is both material and color. There is an eruption of meaning and waves of color, of materials and bodies arising all at once; there is no echo, no time lapse as between lightning and thunder. I think of Italian painters, of Venice, of this stretched canvas, ready to resonate. Ever since the invention of the trampoline canvas, the painter drafts his work before laying onto the canvas successive veils. But through the alchemy of painting, of contours that are both bodies and sheets, traces of the first drawing appear. Paul Klee spent days and days preparing his canvases, creating a space to welcome the sign he would draw in a few minutes. When the sign crosses through thick layers of paint, the process seems to invert our past experiences, dangerously clinging to the vertical face of a painting. The sign rests for a few instants before it escapes when Mark Rothko places us a few centimeters in front of his painting; it travels in this game of successive shudders toward us.

Today meaning resides in us, interpreting and replaying reality, inhabiting this backdrop. And if our lives are positioned under the sign of subtlety we will need to search for the hidden meaning, even if abstraction teaches us that we are the sign we thought we would find.

Pierre David *is a landscape architect practicing in Paris.*

This essay was translated from the French by Danielle Lippoldt and Clotilde Viellard.

Fra Angelico, *Dead Christ,* c. 1440.
Museum of S. Marco, Florence

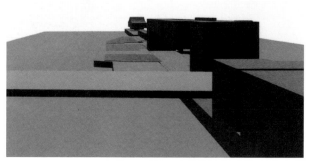

View from Bridge

Florian Beck MArch '97, View from Rowe's Wharf
of Northern Avenue Bridge and Fort Point Channel

Eclogues on the Bay:
Boston—Lido

Homa Fardjadi
Associate Professor of Architecture

Public landscape of experience,
political arena of dialogue, or
intimate space of encounter; food,
swimming, or public exchange
may sound various notes that
coincide to produce the building
of a lido in the city. The site of this
project fronts the bay in Boston.
The city's intricate borders with
water were reviewed in order to
design civic swimming pools and
public buildings.

One conceptual referent for this
project was the still life. In its
recollection of daily life, whether
in Ernst's collages or in Chardin's
paintings, the still life transforms
bodies and things, as though in their
intimate setting, to produce the
uncanny space of the feminine.

Susan Glenn MArch '97, Model View: Fort Point Channel Intervention

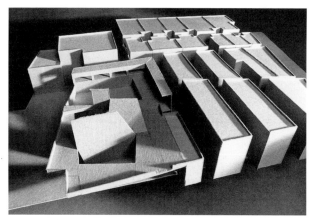

Christina O'Sullivan MArch '97, Conceptual Model of Pool in Site

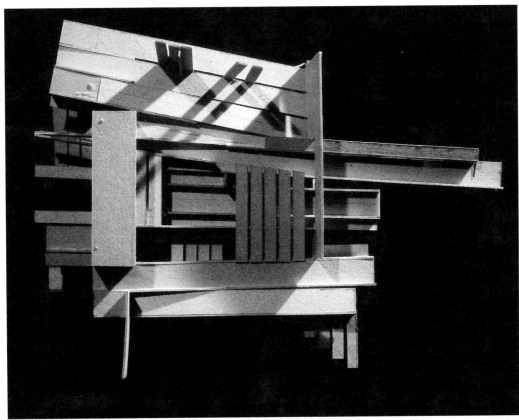

Model Study: Compressed Surface

Model Views: Block and Pool

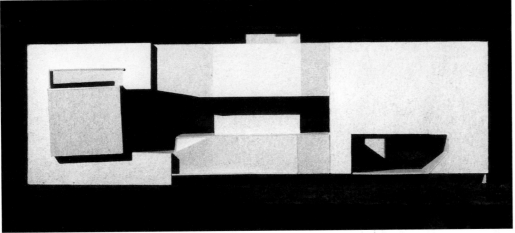

Doris Lim MArch '97, Block Elevation

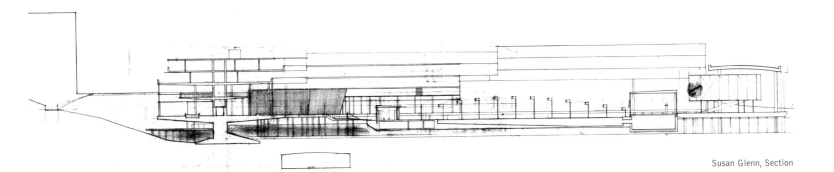

Susan Glenn, Section

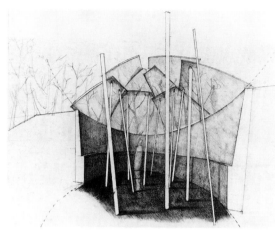

Interior Perspective of Monk's Hut

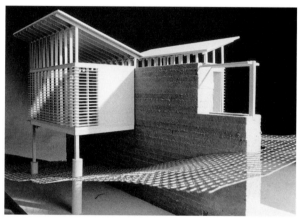
Model Views: Monk's Hut

Spiritual Space

Fred Fisher
Visiting Critic in Architecture

The overwhelming secular and multicultural character of contemporary American culture has eliminated most sources of shared formal meaning. Religious denominational distinctions are increasingly blurred, as are general notions of sacred and profane space. These conditions not withstanding, religious institutions flourish.

The Southeast Asian immigrant population of Southern California has established Buddhist monasteries that function as the traditional interface between society and religion. The quintessential version of this interface is the forest monastery of the Theravada tradition. Monks live in individual huts and gather twice daily for communal meditation. An interchange takes place between the monks, totally dependent for physical needs, and the lay community, which is in turn dependent on the monks for spiritual guidance.

As indicated by its name, the forest monastery is isolated in the natural landscape, separate from the urban fabric. A 60-acre hill situated in an agricultural valley is the site. The facilities include huts for the monks, dormitories for lay visitors, an ordination hall, a group meditation hall, and a dining hall.

Work included a site design, large-scale design of a typical hut, and schematic design of all other structures. A stay on site was recommended and included discussions with the abbot.

Explorations focused on the virtual experience of architecture, metaphoric content, and the integration of landscape with all aspects of the complex.

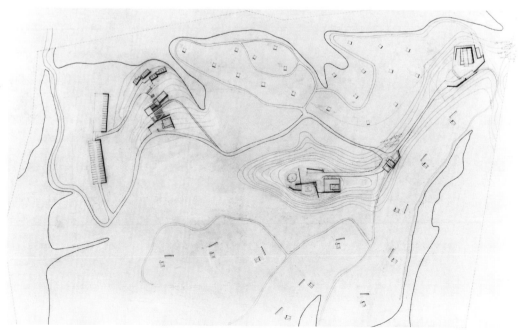

Lisa Huang, MArch '97, Site Plan

Melissa Gorman MArch '97, Model View: Monk's Hut

Craig Roberts MArch '97, Model View: Ordination Hall and Chedi

New Voids

Adriaan Geuze
Visiting Critic in Landscape Architecture

Modern society generates a spin-off of soulless sites of any scale, such as clear-cut forest landscapes, open mines, abandoned industrial zones, and useless city spaces and buildings. The absence of any program or economic initiative gives them no quality except for the beauty of decay. These areas, the New Voids, can be expected to be the contemporary new white spots on the map, real tabulae rasae, ready to be colonized. The project focused on the design and imagination of new structures to initiate new identity, to find culture, to accommodate public life, to improve microclimate and ecological succession, and to provoke a new colonization process on these sites.

Students identified a New Void in either a landscape or a metropolis of America's East Coast. They studied the scale, the physical conditions, the culture of this site and forced a major intervention or a structure to reclaim such an area. Proposals were meant to clarify the new identity, the new texture and spatial quality, or the possible evolution of the site.

The project takes distance from the romantic iconology of landscape architecture and explores the unexploited field in between urban planning, architecture, and landscape architecture.

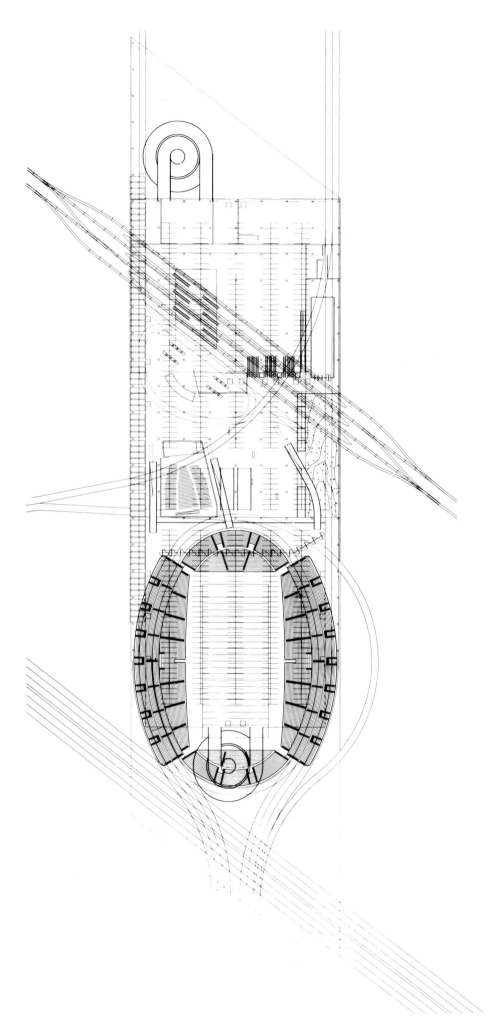

Trevor Bullen MArch '97, A Site on the Massachusetts Turnpike between Worcester and Springfield: Plan

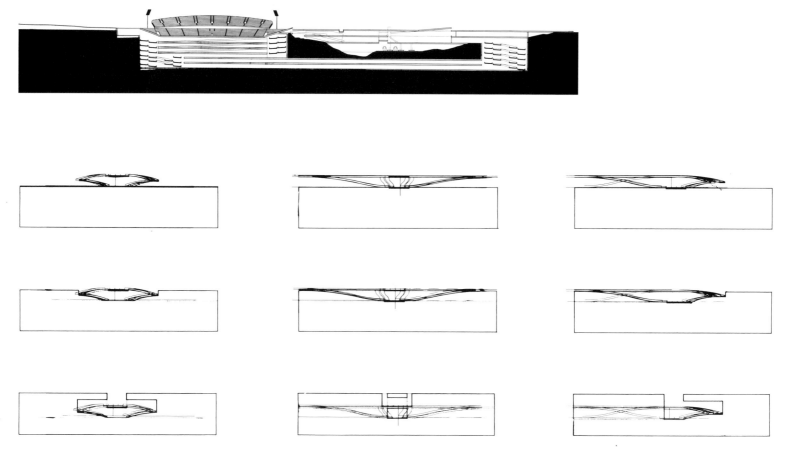

Trevor Bullen, Site Sections

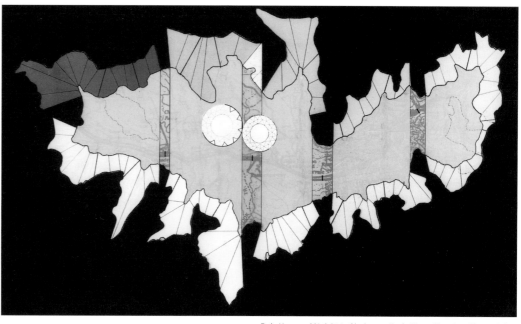

Rob Hopper MLA '96, Chainsaw Park Plan, Showing Clearcutting

Detail View of Elevation

Time Squared: Architecture and Technology

Richard Gluckman and
Jane Wernick
Visiting Critics in Architecture

The subject of this studio is the development of the northeast and southeast corners of 42nd Street and Eighth Avenue. The program is similar to that presented by the New York State Urban Development Corporation. The components of the project include the hotel, retail development, offices, theater, and a cultural center.

The student investigated the relevant linkages with the transportation networks at the subsurface, surface, and elevated condition.

The recent combination of large entertainment companies with news and publishing companies and appliance and technology manufacturers has created a developer/client base that will have a profound effect on planning and architecture. The student considered the "theming" of architectural projects and "co-marketing" of images and products that have generated a language and that integrate image and structure.

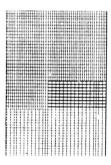

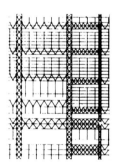

Mihai Craciun MArch '97,
Section Studies

Model Views

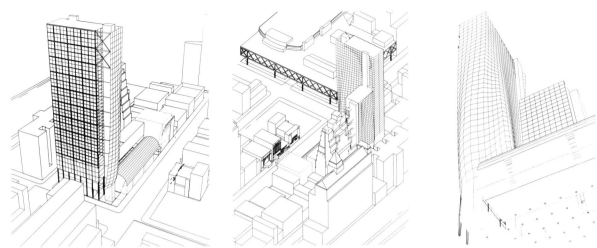

Matthew Littell MArch '97, Axonometric and Perspective Views

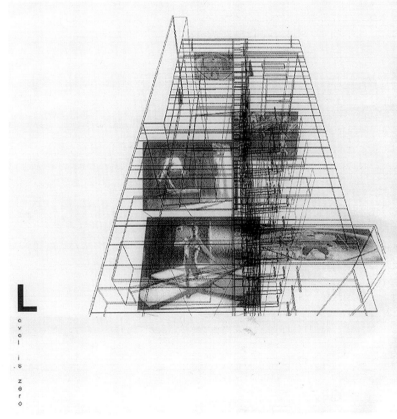

Srdjan Weiss Jovanovic

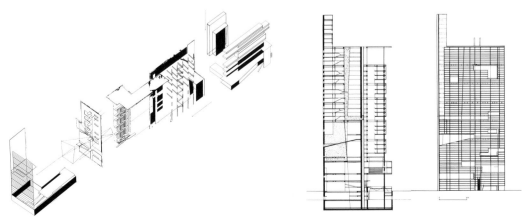

Srdjan Weiss Jovanovic MArch '97, Axonometric, Section, and Elevation

Perspective View

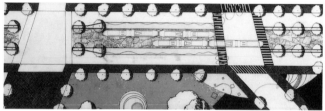

Plan of Park

Washington Street Corridor: Strategic Planning to Revitalize Neighborhoods within a Major Public Transit Corridor

James Kostaras
Visiting Critic in Urban Planning and Design

This studio explored design and planning strategies to encourage and guide urban redevelopment along Boston's Washington Street Corridor. Washington Street, one of the main streets and public transit corridors into downtown Boston, links several diverse neighborhoods, and cuts through a transitional area that has suffered from extensive blight and disinvestment since the 1950s. Vast areas remain undeveloped. The studio was an opportunity to consider new approaches to the revitalization and rebuilding of inner-city districts.

The major challenge of the studio was to meet the following objectives:

• explore ways to optimize the relationship between land use and public transportation;

• guide development on vacant land within the corridor while enhancing the historic architectural character of this area;

• capitalize on public transit and infrastructure investment as a catalyst for urban development and stimulus for private sector investment; and

• consider urban design strategies to rectify the physical failures of 1960s urban renewal planning by weaving together and mending the historic urban fabric disrupted by urban renewal projects.

The studio was divided in two phases: first, students proposed a comprehensive plan, or development strategy, for the entire corridor; in the second phase, students concentrated on a selected area or specific component of their proposed comprehensive plan. Modules in the following areas provided background to the studio: real estate economics, the impact of transportation policy on land use, public finance, and negotiation and consensus-building in the community participation process. Since one of the objectives of the studio was to introduce the community-based planning process, students met during the semester with a task force of residents and business representatives appointed by the Mayor of Boston to focus on the Washington Street Corridor.

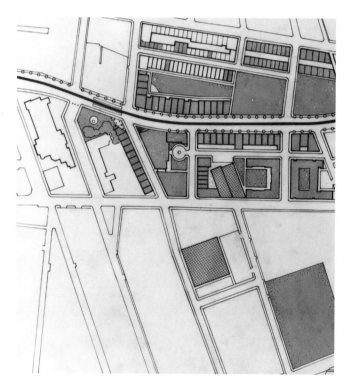

Cathedral Square Site Plan

Jack Hsu MUP '96, Francesca Levaggi MLA '96, and Douglas Manz MUP '96, Elevation of Cathedral Square Proposal

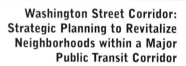

Existing Murals

Perspective Views of Light Rail "Slow Zone"

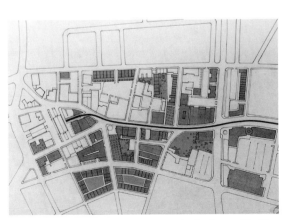

Dudley Square Site Plan

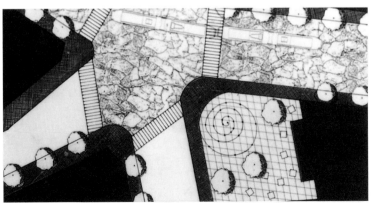

Jack Hsu, Francesca Levaggi, and Douglas Manz, Dudley Square Plan Detail

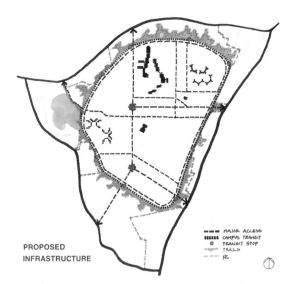

PROPOSED LAND USE

CAMPUS
HOUSING
COMMERCIAL
RECREATIONAL
R&D
OFFICE PARK
RESERVE

PROPOSED
INFRASTRUCTURE

MAJOR ACCESS
CAMPUS TRANSIT
TRANSIT STOP
TRAILS
R.

Wendy Yang MAUD '96, Plan Diagrams

Expanding the Diagram...A Campus Plan for the New Millennium

M. David Lee
Adjunct Professor of Urban Planning and Design

The University of Massachusetts at Dartmouth is a 710-acre campus built on former farmland. The main academic functions are housed within an extraordinary "megastructure" designed in the 1960s by Paul Rudolph. This studio addressed the changing nature of a college campus including expansion needs, universal access, student life issues, and interrelationships with the adjacent community. The studio met with university officials (and student representatives) to understand how the campus currently functions and to develop a physical design program for the future. During the course of the semester, we developed an urban design plan and design criteria for circulation, open space, and building (including new construction and adaptive reuse). In the latter portion of the term, critical elements of the plan were developed in detail. This was an interdisciplinary studio and the work was executed in teams and on an individual basis.

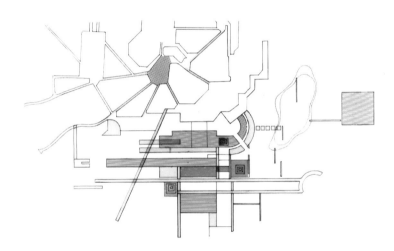

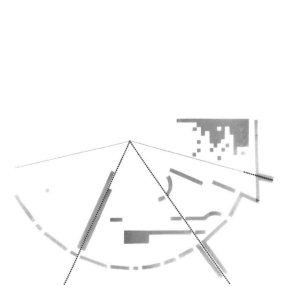

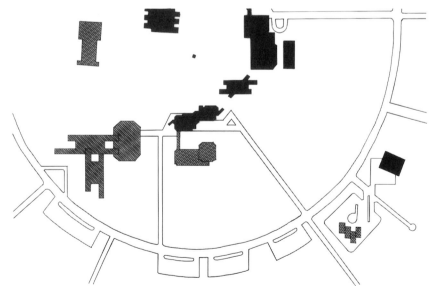

Wen-Shan Huang MLA '96, Plan Diagrams

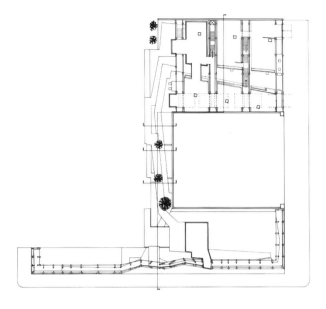

Plan

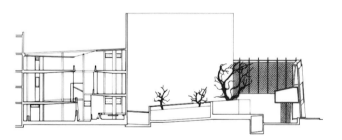

Section Through MoMA Extension Gallery and Bookstore Café

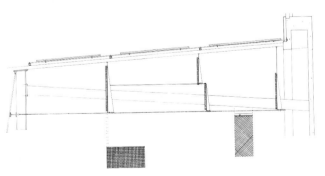

Elizabeth Walker MArch '97, Detail Wall Section

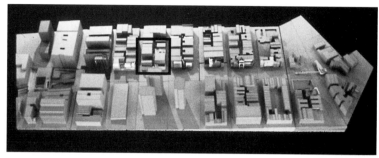

Class Site Model of Houston Street (with project of E. Walker highlighted)

SoHo Masks/Urban Thresholds

Sandro Marpillero
Visiting Critic in Architecture

Architecture is the encounter between the city and the tactile in a specific place and time. What this desired experience is has to be produced every time we make a project. This requires the engagement of both material history and design unconscious with a certain rigor of interpretation and some strategy to heighten one's perception.

This studio was interested in promoting an oscillation between urban and detailed architectural design investigations. Through the reading of both psychoanalytic and surrealist references, conceptual and formal procedures of condensation and displacement were developed as possible techniques of architectural figuration.

The site is ten thin lots at the northern edge of SoHo in Manhattan—the historical trace or scar of the impact of metropolitan scale infrastructures on the compact industrial fabric of what is now landmarked as a "historic district." The challenge posited to the class as a whole was to reengage this faceless strip.

The first part of the semester was spent representing this traumatic urban transformation in its revealed and concealed aspects. This work focused on the production of a design apparatus as analog to the process of individual site construction. Following this, each student produced an architectural project that reinterpreted a chosen urban lot through the materiality of a specific program. Focus was directed toward the definition and design of both exterior and interior building thresholds, as a privileged architectural mode for the critical representation of some of the urban and individual forces that were mapped by each student.

Materials for the studio included short texts of Sigmund Freud and Walter Benjamin, works of Marcel Duchamp, Max Ernst, Paul Klee and individually selected architectural projects. Seminar presentations and discussions of these heterogeneous references were scheduled to complement the stages of development of the design work.

Houston Street as Urban Thesaurus

In this short text, I will limit myself to discussing my approach to the first half of the studio "Sotto Masks/Urban Thresholds." I will begin by pursuing and *italicizing* the (sometimes contradictory) web of synonyms proposed by Roget's *Thesaurus* for the word **approach.**

From the beginning the *Thesaurus,* along with several other "techniques of intention," was used to slow down and open up each student's design approach. As opposed to a dictionary definition, the *Thesaurus* projects topographical possibilities that may lead toward contrasting modes of writing. The associative structure of the *Thesaurus* suggests different techniques of narrative construction, by producing multiple representations of conceptual causation, prospective volition, motions, times, forms, and their corresponding textual orders.

Simon Gathercole, Cambridge Exchange, Site Collage: Refuge and Exposure

The studio interpreted the notion of approach as both *beginning* and *projection into the future*, conceptually identifying the conscious *pursuit of a plan*, and the *accession* to a mode of inquiry. Like words that *invoke* ideas, the architectural figures *encountered* by each student during her/his first visit to Houston Street were *assumed* as *points of departure* toward the *construction* of design *tracks* and architectural *devices*. The studio *addressed* urban concerns within a rigorous *investigation* of design *procedures*. Within the pedagogical sequence of the GSD, option studios mark an intellectual *threshold*, which should *raise* questions of architectural theory through design *practice*. The studio's *intent* was to *promote* the emergence of an independent sensibility, that each student will *carry on*, as s/he *moves* forward in architecture. Projects came about through an experience of *catching oneself* in action at certain conceptually relevant *junctures*. They were then developed in order to *become* both a precise *anticipation* of material constructs and a *probe* about their own *congruent making*. Architectural figuration was thus *acceded to* through significant details that could *make manifest* the whole.

During the first half of the semester, we used references from two fields of cultural production to challenge architecture's load of linguistic conventions, with the goal of decentering predictable modes of design approach. One was Surrealism, the other Freud's writings on the concept of dreamwork. In order to facilitate an approach to the complexity of these references and to offer primary support for the design work, the studio was structured by a series of visual presentations and seminar discussions. Surrealist works by De Chirico, Duchamp, Eluard, Ernst, Giacometti, Klee, and others were first looked at as visual enigmas for their bizarre and contradictory logics, and their manifestation of symbols related to dreamwork processes. Students observed slippages belonging to these artifacts' "unconscious procedures," as discussed by Freud. We examined the Freudian notion of dreamwork as a modality for the production of sense in design, as a paradigmatic strategy for the manifestation of desires, wherein the genetic elaboration of (dream) material is linked to a poetics of the symbolic function. The studio raised questions of how to integrate this paradigm into architecture's multiple practices and realities, bringing into focus similar mechanisms that intervene in the imaginative work of producing a project.

David Yocum MArch '97, Window Machine

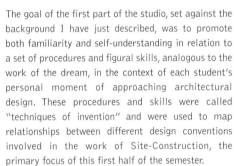

Model: Collapsing Machine

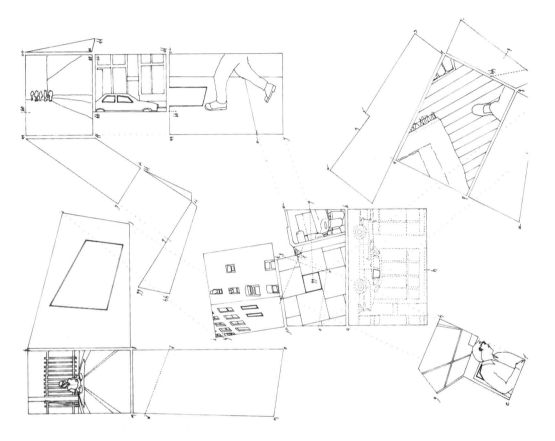

Collapsing Machine: Unfolded Section

The goal of the first part of the studio, set against the background I have just described, was to promote both familiarity and self-understanding in relation to a set of procedures and figural skills, analogous to the work of the dream, in the context of each student's personal moment of approaching architectural design. These procedures and skills were called "techniques of invention" and were used to map relationships between different design conventions involved in the work of Site-Construction, the primary focus of this first half of the semester.

The Site-Construction countered the fiction of objectivity of a conventional analysis phase, by bringing attention to the encounter with a site and the emergence of a model of figural production that addresses the site in terms of formal investigations. Each student was asked to clarify the traumatic or frustrating aspects in his/her chosen site, by producing original ways of looking at it that would formulate her/his intentions. This conceptual experience was not considered as exterior to the "factual" reality of a site, rather helping to mold what is thought of as the "factual." Site-Construction uncovered possible narrative themes, which were read as clues of each site's character and potential. A tension was established between being bound to the concerns of a site and pursuing a free mode of design investigation. This delay of a design's physical closure opened up a site's latent possibilities of inhabitation.

Site-Construction took place through three "techniques of invention," conceptualized as breaks in modes of representation. These three techniques— collage, section, and model—connect disparate materials in a design process and mark the emergence of new figures in that process. Their power resides in their capacity to multiply possibilities and their challenge to each student is the ability to remain true to her/his own emerging experience.

Sandro Marpillero *is an architect practicing in Manhattan. He also teaches architecture at Princeton University and Parsons School of Design.*

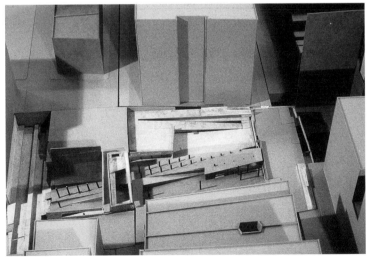

David Yocum, Model View: Intersection of Broadway and Houston

Unwrapped Elevations

G. Anderson Pearson, Liberty Bell Rubbing

A New Home for the Liberty Bell: The Design of Independence Mall, Philadelphia

Larry Mitnick
Visiting Critic in Architecture

The objective of this studio was to design a major public space with national significance. Over the last 50 years, Philadelphia has been developing its Center City through a variety of redevelopment programs and private incentives. As a result of planning strategies primarily developed during the 1950s and very recent initiatives, the plan and the section of the city have undergone major revisions and refinements: not only has the skyline become more predominant as height restrictions increased, but the subterranean level throughout Center City has also developed into a network of underground streets and shops connecting transportation systems. The subterranean level has special significance to the city as it reveals, through light and sound, archaeological and stratified conditions that constitute Philadelphia's historical identity.

The program included an analysis of the existing site and the artifact, the Liberty Bell; careful consideration of the sequence between major historical sites (Independence Hall, Liberty Bell, and the Mall); a new Constitution Center; a new home for the Liberty Bell; and the development of public open spaces and park areas.

Bell Mold

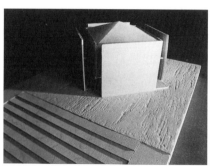

G. Anderson Pearson MArch '97, Bell Pavilion Model View

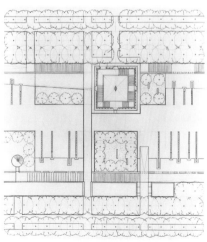

Jennifer Brooke, Site Plan Detail

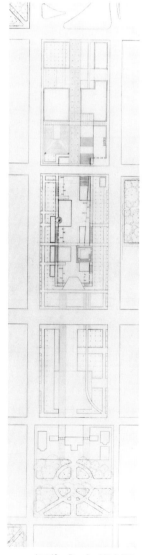

Jennifer Brooke MLA '96, Site Plan: Independence Mall Model View

Independence Hall
Liberty Bell
Chestnut Street
Free Quaker Meeting House
Subway Station
Market Street
Cemetery
Philadelphia
Horse and Buggy
Arch Street
Judge Lewis Quadrangle
Brick Arcades
Virginia
New York
Massachusetts
Connecticut
Rhode Island
New Hampshire
Maryland
New Jersey
North Carolina
South Carolina
Pennsylvania
Delaware
Georgia
Tree
Park Bench
Marble Step
Glass Pavilion
Pigeon
Bus
Newsstand
Underground Garage
Fifth Street
Taxi
Lamp Post
Garden
Water Fountain
Bronze Engraving
Chiseled Stone
Embossed Concrete
Garden Wall
Raised Letter
Cast Iron Fence
Grave
Name
Date
First Bank
Sixth Street
Ben Franklin Bridge
Metal Lock
Masonry Joint
Flemish Bond
Stroller
Tourist
Worker
Camera
Concession Stand
Men's Toilet
Women's Toilet
Parent
Child
Elderly
Map
Ticket
Drain
Merchants Exchange
Planter
Chair
Kiosk
Fire Hydrant
Radio
Lines
Hot Dog
Water
Italian Ice
Pretzel
Flag
US Mint
Picnic Table
Gate
Delaration (Graff) House
Second Bank
Mulch
Flower Bed
Garbage Can
Motorized Trolley
Metal Flagpole
Paver
Sewer Cover
Memorial

No ideas but in things
W.C. Williams [1]

Images reveal nothing to the lazydreamer
G. Bachelard [2]

With feet solidly planted on earth we enter our design process through investigations of the real; a study of concrete reality of both site and object. We accept reality as a necessary angel. Through perception we record what appears to be a stable and completely realized image. However, while a dry listing of what we experience may be evocative to an imaginative mind, it is the recognition that, as Bachelard has said, "the imaginary is immanent in the real,"[3] that fuels our curiosity. Soon the stability of the images we find out there is transformed. We begin to draw out from our perception of the real, a desire and an aspiration toward new images. The physical world becomes a point of departure from which the immense structures of the imagination are erected. In this sense, objects (through perception) are given immediately or intuited. In other words, no boundary exists between ourselves and the thing.

A really close reading of an object forces us to investigate the particular through which we discover the universal. Using drawing techniques that investigate section and sectional overlays, x-ray, projection systems, as well as models using paper, cardboard, wood, metal, plaster, we learn to see. We also learn to appreciate precision. Furthermore, to be engaged in a process of actually making objects, grounds us in the material condition of our own making. We draw strength from the limitations of our craft; the objects and spaces we make must take concrete form—whether as drawing, model, or built work. We cannot rise to higher, more 'abstract' realms; we must accept the inevitable—the feeling of joy and of melancholy because we cannot go beyond this very simple fact.

The student is taught that authentic selfhood can only be lived, not thought. The student encounters the self not in detachment of thought, but in the involvement and paths of choice.

And out of what one sees and hears and out of what one feels, who could have thought to make so many selves, so many sensuous worlds.
W. Stevens[4]

Making through participation (methexis) and transformation of material through technique, allows for a record of choices to transpire. Giving oneself up to the process of making allows one to find the universal in the process itself. In fact, this kind of learning, based on techne offers one a special and privileged stance, a special knowledge.

It is through things, found and made, rather than ideas that we seek a poetic dimension. 'Objets à réaction poetique' create reverberations between inner and outer qualities obliterating any absolute separation between objective and subjective experience. Collecting things, the list grows longer and in a sense this very listing decomposes reality. Through a collision of objects, or unlikely combination of broken metaphors the architect produces an ambivalence, a multiplicity or polyvalence that goes beyond reality and lays bare the imagination. Faced with the accompanying enigma, we are invited to dream.

Larry Mitnick *is Professor of Architecture at the University of the Arts in Philadelphia.*

1. William Carlos Williams, *Selected Poems,* edited by Charles Tomlinson (New York: New Directions, 1985), xii

2. Gaston Bachelard, *On Poetic Imagination and Reverie,* translated with an introduction by Colette Gaudin (Indianapolis: Bobbs-Merrill, 1971), xxvii

3. Bachelard, *Air and Dreams* (Dallas: Dallas Institute of Humanities and Culture, 1988), 4.

4. Helen Hennessy Vendler, *On Extended Wings*: Wallace Stevens' longer poems, (Cambridge, MA: Harvard University Press, 1969), 51.

Views of Conceptual Massing Model (Positive and Negative)

In The Tank

Eric Owen Moss
Visiting Critic in Architecture

Four neoclassical masonry tanks, built at the end of the nineteenth century, stand empty near the airport in Vienna. Once used for gas storage, the four domed cylinders—60 meters in diameter, 65 meters high—are used only for an occasional concert or social event. 15,000 square meters of high-rise apartments will be built in each tank along with 5,000 square meters of retail, parking, and a rock concert hall. The Vienna lighting code, which prescribes natural light for living units, is applicable.

Larry Burks MArch '97, Model View

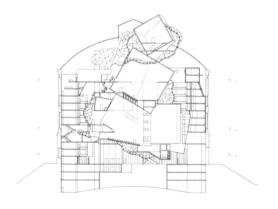

Olivia Cheung MArch '97,
Section through Concert Hall and Hotel

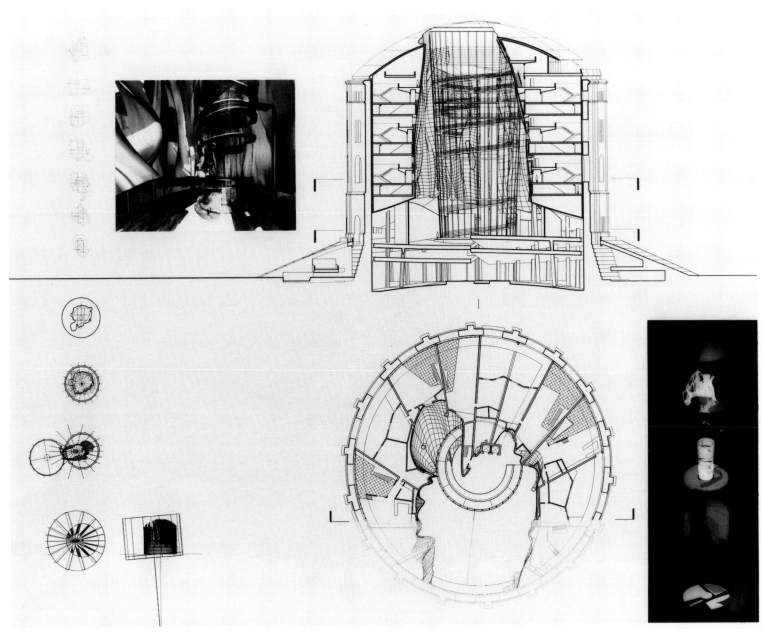

Larry Burks, Plan Diagrams, Perspective View of Interior Courtyard, Courtyard Section

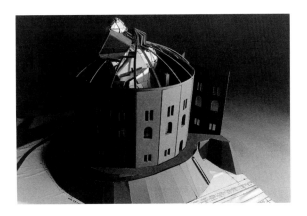

Olivia Cheung, Sectional Model Views

Yuyang Liu MArch '97, Model View

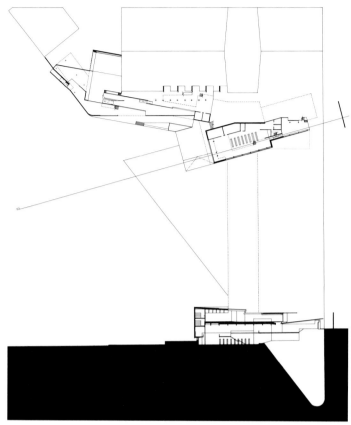

Plan/Section

Constructing Site

John and Patricia Patkau
Visiting Critics in Architecture

Bounded on all sides by the urban amenities of downtown Vancouver, the West End is unique in Canada for its dense residential neighborhood of point towers. Its population is approximately 49,300 people per square mile (compared to Boston at about 11,860 people). While the area has excellent proximity to downtown offices, shopping, theater, night life, beaches, Stanley Park (the major city park), plus some of the best "views" in the city, these amenities, in general, are seen to belong to the greater Vancouver district. Internally, the West End lacks important public infrastructure. It needs both a new library and an additional high school as well as community facilities for various groups and activities, additional small-scale park space, community workshop space to serve the apartment population, etc. According to city policy, this area is rapidly approaching its limit of development. Few developable sites remain and these are generally controlled by private interests. If the West End is to meet its public needs for space, it will have to rethink the idea of site in a way that makes space for the public in this already condensed fabric.

Physically, the site of the West End is a form of "walled" city. These walls have been constructed over the years in an attempt to divert heavy downtown traffic around the area's boundaries. The walls are constructed of speed bumps, street closures, diversions, and round-abouts. These devices have provided certain amenities for the West End simply by consequence, that is, unintentionally—small public parks at the scale and dimension of the street, etc. No attempt has been made to rethink these spaces in terms of a typology of the area. One spatial type, park, is simply substituted for another, street.

This studio looked at the spatial infrastructure of the West End in an attempt to define "other" notions of site, notions that might see site as other than city plat. To do this it was necessary that certain traditional jurisdictions be questioned. The work called for strategies that cross various jurisdictions, controls, and disciplinary boundaries to "think" the city as an integrated possibility. Through the vehicle of a particular neighborhood and project, students were asked to investigate the spatial infrastructure of the city for its potential to provide for the "public" in nontraditional ways.

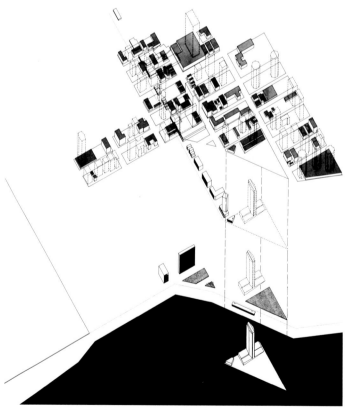

Hao Ko MArch '97, Axonometric Showing Intersections of Urban Systems

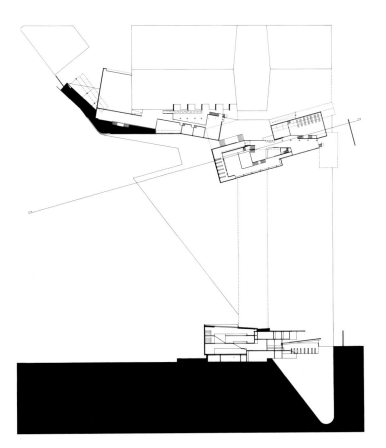
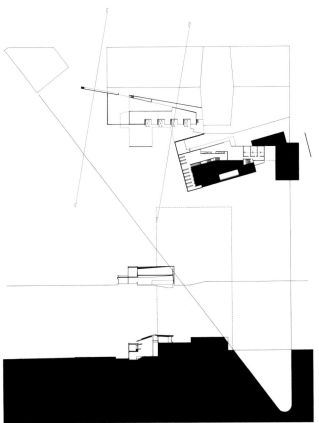

Plans/Sections Through Library

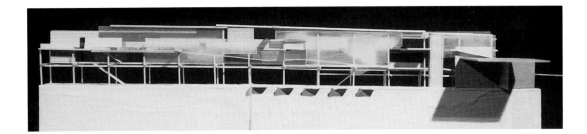

Yuyang Liu, Model Views

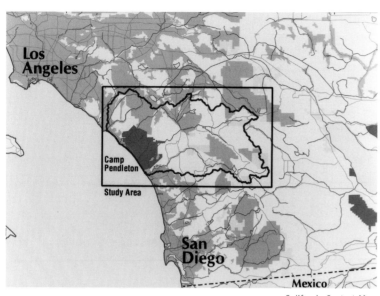

California Context Map

Alternative Futures for the Context Region of Camp Pendleton, CA

Carl Steinitz
Alexander and Victoria Wiley Professor of Landscape Architecture and Planning

Allan Shearer
Teaching Fellow

Representation
In order to evaluate the dynamic processes at work in the study area, a computer-based Geographic Information System was designed to contain digital data describing the study area. The final study data base is in the form of 12 million "raster" grid cells at a uniform resolution of 30M square. In addition, a number of linear features were maintained as a linear "vector" data base. "Models" were developed to evaluate the landscape and produce a series of maps representing any time-stage.

Process
The state of landscape is the result of many processes, both cultural and natural.

Evaluation
Each of the component process models is used to evaluate the "base-state landscape." For example, the visual quality model assesses regional preferences for landscape views in the study area. The soils models evaluate erodability and the agricultural productivity of the area's soils. The hydrology models predict the 100-year storm hydrographs for each of the rivers and their subwatersheds, flooding heights and water discharge, as well as resultant soil moisture. The fire models assess the needs for fire to maintain vegetation habitat, as well as the risks of fire and fire suppression. The vegetation model assesses vegetation-rarity, as well as providing a basis for species-habitat relationships. Biodiversity is being assessed in three ways: a) via landscape ecological pattern and function, b) via selected single species potential habitat models, and c) via species richness GAP analysis modeling.

Change
Future change is simulated via the "buildout" of six alternative projections for the study region. Alternatives #1 and #2 are based upon the current local and regional plans as summarized by SCAG and SANDAG. Alternative #2 also assumes the implementation of conservation programs and the application of a set of development constraints to wetlands and steep slopes.

Four additional projections for the urbanization of the study region were designed by the studio participants. They reflect alternative development and conservation policies. Alternative #3 illustrates what may be considered the dominant trend: extensive, low-density growth. Alternative #4 also follows the low density trend, but as a means to conserve biodiversity. Alternative #5, focusing on cluster development and new communities, and Alternative #6, concentrating growth in a new urban center, also aim to accommodate growth while maintaining biodiversity.

Impact
Each process model assesses the impact caused by the changes in each alternative.

Decision
The alternative future scenarios may be used by stakeholders, including M.C.B Camp Pendleton, to assess the desirability of the various policies which generated them. The models may also be used to devise and subsequently compare the desirability of additional development scenarios and conservation strategies.

Patricia Bales MLA '96
David Barnard MAUD '96
Hilary Bidwell MLA '96
Jorgen Blomberg MLA '96
Derek Bowser MLA'96
Jonathan Crowder MLA '96
Debra Friedman MLA '96
Kenneth Goldsmith MUP '96
Gwang Ya Han MAUD '96
Bert Hoffman MUP '96
Martin Mildbrandt MLA '96
Koa Pickering MLA '96
Hillary Quarles MLA '96
Carrie Steinbaum MLA '96
Atsushi Tsunekawa (Visiting Scholar)
Robert Winstead MArch '97
Ephrat Yovel MDesS '96

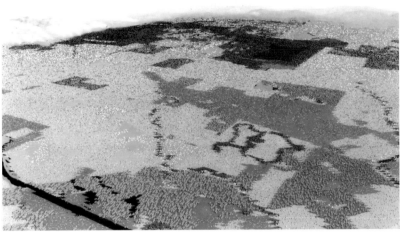

Trend Buildout without Conservation

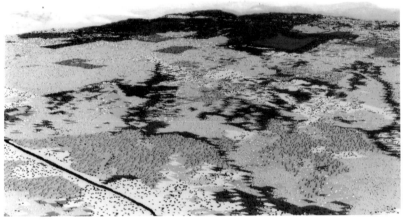

Trend Buildout with Conservation

Private Conservation Buildout

Multi-Centers Buildout

Conductors Versus Soloists

The vast majority of professional education in landscape architecture is directed at educating soloists. Despite the entry-level employment toward which most students aim—employment that can be be characterized as being neither similar to a soloist nor similar to a conductor—I submit that most students see themselves as becoming soloists. Their goal is to master all of the skills and knowledge needed for effective professional activity—to identify problems, analyze them, design solutions, and see them built to the satisfaction of self, client, and peer. This attitude is not just egocentric, it is a reflection of our design education system and a central product of that system.

We are all familiar with the traditional format and structure of studio-based education in which a problem statement is given, students typically work as individuals, and their work is reviewed by expert juries in a somewhat competitive and defensive presentation format. We have all participated in this process as students or as faculty and I suspect that we all have an understanding of the great strengths of this system and of some of its weaknesses. Some of the survivors of this teaching method do indeed become highly effective soloists. Many, probably the majority, remain useful 'second trombonists' throughout their careers. My purpose is not to attack the traditional studio system upon which most of our schools base their education. Rather, it is to ask another question: where do the conductors come from?

Relatively few students see their long-term objectives as preparing themselves for conducting—for being the leaders or managers of teams that share an enterprise and the responsibilities for its success or failure. Yet a surprising number of the students whom I have taught in the past are now in professional practice as conductors. They are partners and associates in larger firms functioning as leaders of project teams. They are in policy-making levels of public agencies. Some of them are teachers. Their professional success is due as much to their critical, judgmental, and managerial skills as it is to their actual design and production capabilities. All too frequently they have undergone a difficult and sometimes painful transition between the roles for which they were initially trained and in which they entered the profession, and their current roles, which tend to involve more responsibility and possibly less direct involvement with design activities.

Over the past years I have taught a considerable number of courses that have been organized in a manner requiring students to work in teams, frequently in large multidisciplinary teams. The reasons are many but normally center upon the scope and complexity of the problem around which the studio is focused and the need for many individual tasks to be coordinated. Sometimes teams have been as small as three persons, and sometimes they have involved a studio class of 15 to 18 persons. The majority of my students have had some team experiences prior to taking my studio, but those experiences have not always been clearly organized, and frequently they have not been socially or productively successful.

My studios are invariably focused on a large and highly valued landscape region experiencing considerable pressures for change. The studio is organized in a manner analogous to a large office team, with the students themselves being largely responsible for the entire project. Students are responsible for problem identification, methodological approach, production and presentation of work, and all aspects of project management including budget allocation. The faculty responsibilities are diverse but emphasize the roles of producer, consultant, and presence. The sociology of the class is very different from the traditional design studio in terms of student/faculty and student/student relationships. The educational experience is also different.

Students volunteer knowing that the project will be organized by them and that it may involve them functioning as a large team. It is also made clear to the students that even though they are in my studio, I consider this to be their project.

An initial field trip is crucial to the definition of the study and to the creation of an effective working team. The organization of that field trip is the first studio task. Issues associated with how a team attacks an area with which it is only vaguely familiar are important ones to resolve. Studio managers, who change monthly, are responsible for the assignment of research responsibilities, be they functional, systematic, or geographic. They manage budget allocation and they organize all logistics.

The field trip is an intensively scheduled working session with both group and individual responsibilities. Without question, the work tasks associated with becoming familiar with issues, geography, and people are of prime importance. The entire group meets every evening and there is a high level of debriefing and other communications. The management group must be adaptable to unforeseen circumstances and must be prepared to make immediate assignment decisions.

Of critical importance during the field trip is the absence of any attempt to define the study. I make a point of telling the students that we are on the field trip to observe and ask questions, but not to decide anything. I do not want the students to informally negotiate the scope and responsibilities of the project. This will be an early task upon return to Cambridge, after a few days of reflection and incubation.

Back at Harvard, the first phase of developing the detailed work plan for the study is the only part of the semester that I organize. First, participants diagram, write, or describe how they see the project developing. What are its objectives, proposed methodologies, and products? In a silent review, each student ranks each presentation for similarity to his or her own ideas. Then, on the basis of similarity (and not personality, skill, or experience) teams are formed for a one-week exercise in proposal preparation. At the end of that week each team presents a written proposal for the entire study, describing objectives, methodology, product, budget, etc. The proposals are publicly reviewed by a panel including myself, a representative from the study area, and outside faculty and professionals. The review is conducted in the presence of the students but without their active participation, as though it were an expert panel conducting an evaluation review. The proposals are ranked and those rankings and comments are publicly communicated to the students. The next class meeting is a negotiation in which the students, having seen the range of ideas and the comments, negotiate (usually in a friendly manner) the critical path of the project. This occurs about two weeks into the semester and results in a study plan in which all of the issues have been publicly decided and to which all participants can willingly commit themselves. For the students, the questions of 'what to do' and 'how to proceed' are recognized as being complex practical choices rather than theoretical inevitabilities.

Having decided what to do, the student managerial roles come into ascendancy again. Clearly, the success of self-management depends upon shared objectives and a shared project design. It also depends upon some roles and social rules that must be openly discussed, understood, and accepted. These have benefits but they also have costs. As part of the study plan, management responsibilities are assigned for the entire semester-long project period. Everybody takes a responsibility in the management committee for at least a month. Everybody has a turn to be a conductor. There is a need for constant communication. Each studio day begins with a class meeting, chaired on a rotating basis by a member of the management committee. All collective business, reporting, reviewing, assignment, and any special seminars and consulting presentations take place at the class meeting. The management committee generally brings all major questions to the whole class for discussion, along with a recommended course of action. Normally, decisions are made by consensus rather than a voting procedure. Work and budget discussions are frequent in the class meetings and the student chairperson of that meeting is in a role not unlike the managing partner in an office who is reviewing the progress of a large project. At the end of every managerial phase, which is typically also the end of a major project work phase, the managerial team presents a 'state of the project' report to the class, including its assessment of progress, quality, and budget.

It is obvious that one of the costs of this approach is that each student cannot and does not do all tasks, even though each student participates in each phase of the study. Accordingly, students are encouraged to make presentations of their individual work that may be of interest to others. The documentation of the study also serves this broadening purpose. At the end of the study the full range of project documents are compiled into a single document for each student. Another important shared responsibility is that of public communication and presentation.

A considerable amount of innovative and high quality work results from these team-oriented studios, despite the fact that students are placed in an unfamiliar situation for which their previous education has not fully prepared them. A major reason for this success is self-motivation and peer pressure associated with the fact that both credit and blame are part of their own sense of accomplishment and self-confidence.

While we should continue to train soloists for their essential roles in the design professions, our educational institutions should recognize the differences in education, style, and skill required of conductors. Nobody should escape at least some education directed toward the roles of the conductor, not only because there are a large number of crucial design problems that require team approaches, but also because a lack of exposure to conducting roles can seriously hinder our students' future professional careers.

Carl Steinitz *is Alexander and Victoria Wiley Professor of Landscape Architecture and Planning at the GSD. His teaching and research are devoted to improving the methods by which planners and designers organize and analyze information about large land areas and how they make major design decisions.*

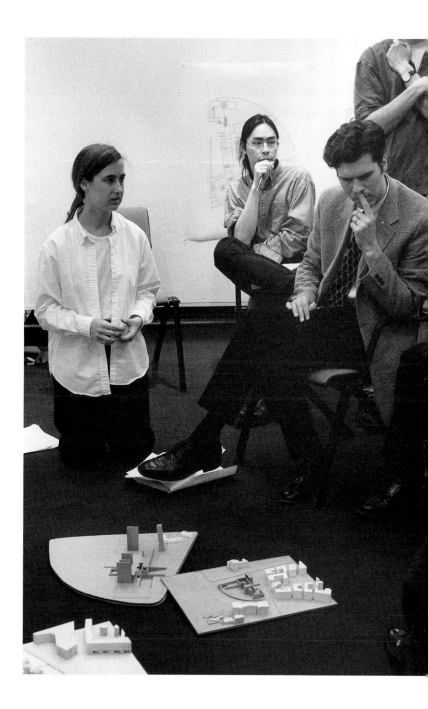

Bronzeville Roundtable

This discussion explores 'approaches' within and across disciplinary boundaries, highlighting work from two studios, taught as a series, and characterized by several key aspects: the multi-disciplinary nature of both the project and the students, group work, the public nature of the projects, and the variety of end-products. The presentation includes excerpts from a discussion, held May 22, 1996, between six of the students in Bronzeville I and seven of the students in Bronzeville II with the student editors of *SW4*. A written commentary by Lee Cott, appears on page 62, immediately following the studio work from his fall semester Bronzeville studio.

Students from Lee Cott's studios Bronzeville I (BI) and II (BII) discuss questions implied by the nature of the studio projects, the particular approaches of the individual students, within and across disciplines :

Rachel Goldsmith (**RG**) BII

Benjamin Gilmartin (**BG**) BI

Edith Hsu-Chen (**EH**) BII

Christopher Keane (**CK**) BI

Lillian Kuri (**LK**) BII

Samuel Lasky (**SL**) BI

Catherine Melina (**CM**) BII

Joseph Minicozzi (**JM**) BII

Gretchen Schneider (**GS**) BI

Brent Stringfellow (**BS**) BII

Gregory Taylor (**GT**) BII

Derrick Woody (**DW**) BI & BII

moderated by *Studio Works 4* Student Editors

Rose Brady (**RB**)

and Jay Berman (**JB**)

"Bronzeville I: 35th Street—A Street in Bronzeville" and "Bronzeville II: The Revitalization of Stateway Gardens Public Housing" were offered through the Department of Urban Planning and Design by Lee Cott. Bronzeville II was taught jointly with real estate consultant and architect Richard Graf. The site of both studios was the Stateway Gardens Housing neighborhood on Chicago's South Side. The focus of Bronzeville I was the development of urban design strategies for neighborhood revitalization, while the intent of Bronzeville I was the development of urban design strategies for neighborhood revitalization, while the intent of Bronzeville II was to investigate the particular relationship between design and real estate economics for the renewal of large-scale public housing. Both studios were conducted in collaboration with the College of Architecture at the Illinois Institute of Technology. Students from IIT and GSD worked simultaneously on similar studio projects and participated in neighborhood meetings and presentations in Chicago.

DW   Having been in both studios I would say that this semester's studio was probably more difficult and more exhausting than the fall semester studio. I'm exhausted.

    RB   Why is that?

    DW   Why? In dealing with a commercial strip (the focus of BI) there's more flexibility than in dealing with people's lives, which is what we were dealing with, in part, this semester. One of the things that all of us realized at the beginning of the semester—given that we were going to be talking with the residents from Stateway Gardens—was that there might be expectations from the residents in terms of the end product of the studio. I think that they came to the first and second meetings with those expectations. That set up a situation where we were in a way responsible in terms of the designs that we actually presented to them.

RB   Perhaps we can open up the discussion regarding the public nature of these studios, and how that affected each studio. Did it change the work that you were doing? Did it strike you as markedly different from other studios because of that particular aspect?

BS   Now when you say public, do you mean socially or do you just mean the fact that it's...

RB   Clients. That one has a certain client? Maybe part of the studios was defining that for yourselves. So what did it mean to you?

BS   The chance to take part in a studio that engaged issues of the inner city such as poverty, racism, American culture, social awareness, and action was important.

    DW   At the same time that I was taking this studio (BII) I was taking Rosalyn Deutsche's seminar "Questions of Public Space." Throughout the semester we tried to figure out what the word "public" meant, and who it included and who it excluded, and over the course of the semester I wasn't so sure whether this was really public housing, because if you look at the definition of "public" it means participatory, being actively involved in some sort of process, as a group. And I don't really believe that society collectively has been involved in the lives of these children and men and women who live at Stateway Gardens. So I'm hesitant about calling it the public. You look at the demographics and they don't really represent the public of Chicago, or the public of the United States. They represent poor people who just happen to be African-American. And throughout the rest of the Chicago Housing Authority housing, they represent minorities in general. They don't represent the public.

    JB   Was the definition of "public" and what it meant to individuals different by discipline? I'd also like to hear comments regarding the program specifically.

LK   I think the nature of the task made it equally difficult for all the students. It became apparent at our final review, when the jury didn't comment on the kind of the drawings that we had produced, or any of the work at the end, because across the board the kind of things that we needed to discuss were not really in any of our disciplines. It was more about economics and social programs and other things that weren't our expertise. So it was difficult.

DW   I kind of challenge that, in that we're architects and we're dealing with a wide range of people from a wide range of backgrounds economically and socially. We have to at least be conversant in these subjects.

LK   Conversant is one thing. But it was as if the kind of things we were proposing, we really didn't know that much about. I mean, even though it was good to be able to speak about them, the things that we knew best, designing or planning or whatever, weren't things we were using as tools.

BS   It seems as if, because we were entering an area that the majority of us were unfamiliar with, that much of the time was taken up in finding out what this was about. The idea of forming strong positions through which you actually have an interaction and a debate about these issues was, to a certain degree, impossible, because everybody was on such uncertain ground for a long period of time; you never had the chance to actually sit down, and as a planner or as an architect or as a landscape architect say "well, this is what I've seen, this is how I think about it, and this is what I'm going to propose." And I think we didn't have enough time to actually get to the point where we could start to have those solid grounds through which a debate could ensue.

EH   It was obvious to us all that this issue is much more than just design or planning. I think we all realized that this has to be more than an interdisciplinary undertaking within the GSD. This can involve other schools here at Harvard. We did have a few seminars with members of the Education School, the Public Health School, and the Business School. But they could have been more integral in the process, even having some student participation from the Kennedy School. I mean, all these factors contribute to the public housing problem, not just design, not just planning.

RG   I agree with Edith. I definitely support the forum of the studio as a place in which these kinds of problems should be dealt with. But I think if we're going to talk about doing an interdisciplinary studio and looking at this from all the different perspectives from which it needs to be addressed, we have to really do that. This studio, this spring, was called a real estate development studio, and it had little, if anything, to do with real estate development. I thought it had more to do with community economic development. If we're going to do these interdisciplinary studios then we really need to actually have a public health person, have a planner there, have an architect there, have somebody from HUD there.

DW   Around midterm I was speaking with Professor Cott, and one of the things that I told him was that maybe there should have been, like, a Bronzeville 2A in which, for that second semester with that second course in the series, the students would research specific topics that were relevant for the tenant. And then in the following semester, Bronzeville 2B, there would have been the design application of it, i.e., what we did this semester in studio, in terms of applying the information that had been gathered and developing some sort of design critique. And that could be used or handed over to the residents as a more realistic kind of strategy for redevelopment.

the kind of things that we needed to discuss were not really in any of our disciplines. It was more about economics and social programs and other things that weren't our expertise

—LK

RB So in terms of their expectations, would you say that the community was, as a result of the first-semester studio, expecting something that they didn't receive? Or that there was a gap in the development of the studio or the studio program, the one-year studio project? That in a sense that there was some expectation that wasn't met?

DW I don't think we really gave them what they wanted. I mean, we went there with the intention of studying these people, and these people have been studied a lot in recent years and they're quite fed up with it right now. And I think a lot of us realized that between the first and second meeting. And what they wanted was to know why we were there to begin with, and then some sort of process or some help in determining what they could get from our involvement.

> *We need to show an investment in the community if we're going to go out there.*
>
> **—GT**

GS We had two different audiences with each semester. First semester we had a pretty clear client—the Mid-South Planning Commission—and we were giving them a document at the end of the semester. We also met with the 35th Street Merchants Association. And although we did go to the City Hall, on our first meeting in Chicago our interaction was much closer and clearly aligned to the community and the merchants and the planners in the community. So in the second semester, from my understanding, you weren't dealing with the merchants and the planners so much, you were dealing with residents.

BS There was a certain undefined quality as to who we were dealing with in the second semester, and I think that was one of the fundamental flaws [of the studio]. The idea, first of all, that it would be a real world process was undermined by the fact that we never took a real world approach, nor did we retreat into a traditional academic position where we operated independently and gathered information and formed an opinion out of that. And so we were stuck in this middle ground where we had a certain confused relationship with HUD, with the residents, and with the CHA [Chicago Housing Authority]. In the end (and I thought this was very clear and up front in our reviews) it was unclear where this fit into the academic process. I think that's a great challenge for these type of studios, which try to offer this real world experience: defining themselves when they are operating as an extension of the academy.

GT I think we also, in going to Chicago, especially two semesters in a row, raised a lot of suspicions as to why we were making this effort to travel that far. It was asked of us at our first meeting with the residents: "you have areas within Boston that could be addressed, why are you coming to Chicago?" That was never really fully defined. I think Harvard as an institution should really question and look at what we have here in our own community. Either that, or make a longer-term commitment there. We need to show an investment in the community if we're going to go out there.

RG   We have to be clear about who the client is in these kinds of situations. That wasn't really made clear this semester. Making a commitment to a client is a pretty funny thing to think about when you might say that we are the clients. That sounds crass, but it's our tuition that's involved and we're here for an education. To a certain extent that involves case studies. But are we going to make these people into a case study or are they our client?

CK   Your allegiance is torn between learning something and doing something that may not be what you might typically get out of an academic exercise. On the other hand, I think that one thing that I have gotten out of this experience, regardless of the final product, has to do with what we were talking about before: defining what the role of the design profession is in relation to all these problems. Clearly everyone here and everyone in the school thinks that there is a role to be played. But it may not be the case any more that that role is fixing a problem through design. It may be a smaller portion of that.

It seems to me that this studio was no different from any other studio at the GSD. We had no real world powers. We had no efficacy.

—SL

LK   In our studio (BII) I learned a lot more from going to Chicago and from the process [which resulted], because it was an interdisciplinary studio dealing with a very difficult problem. It was different from any other studio where you end up learning most from the critique, which really didn't happen in our studio.

CK   In the end you want the final product for yourself to mean something. To me that was not necessarily learning how to design better, but learning about how things like this should be dealt with. But as soon as you have a client you're kind of obligated to have something of value at the end, and I don't know how possible that is in this kind of situation.

JM   A lot of the confusion we saw is what happens when there are politics involved—different people who have different controls. Too often in a studio, we say this is my problem and this is my answer. But it's more cloudy than that, and I think that was what threw us off a little bit, or a lot, actually.

JB   Does anybody want to conjecture what this same studio would have been like if it were like a typical studio offered in architecture school, where the people who see your results aren't the people for whom it's being done?

SL   It seems to me that that this studio was no different from any other studio at the GSD. We went out there, we did the little field research, we talked to maybe 10 of the 50 merchants, maybe 20 residents of the 1,200. You can hardly say that there was any full-scale research done. We had no real world powers. We had no efficacy. It could only be a real world studio if you were living in Chicago, where you are in touch with various officials and different agencies. I think that it's reasonable to assume that if you were on the Chicago end of things you would have the expectation that the students held a certain amount of actual power, that we in fact didn't ever hold.

LK   I kind of disagree. Our studio felt responsibility to the client and that made us start thinking about how really complex this has been. Sometimes when you're disconnected from something you can produce very interesting things. And the more you get involved, it actually gets more difficult. I think we didn't get extremely involved but we did reach a point where it was really affecting us.

BS   I would say at least it's starting to open a slight bit of consciousness. Had we approached the problem without going to Chicago, without meeting with anybody, without having to deal with the actual agencies that were involved, [this consciousness] might not have existed.

SL   My point is more that if this were a real world situation, there would have been less time to question and you would have been forced by the schedule to make decisions and let the chips fall where they may. That's exactly what happened before. Someone said "we have a problem, we're going to try and solve it." Someone said "we'll build the Stateway Gardens," and it turned out to be a disaster. So, it failed. If we had truly been employed, we would have had to deal more with the consequences of our choices. Because we didn't have that option to move the project along, we sort of wallowed in the world of "well, what if we did this?"

RB   Do you think it's possible to create an actual client/consultant relationship in the studio environment?

SL   I don't think CHA [Chicago Housing Authority] is going to cede its control to a bunch of architecture students at the GSD.

RB   Does the studio then have to be structured as simulated "real world"?

SL   No, but I think [it might be necessary] to say to people: "This is an academic exercise. Of course we're concerned with what's going on out here, otherwise we wouldn't be doing this, but you have to understand that we don't have power." I think that if that understanding were in the minds of people in Chicago, then in a certain sense that would free us up to act, because we wouldn't always be thinking of how they were going to view what was done. Because they might be more open minded.

BS   I don't think it's an issue of us having power or not. It's an issue of us empowering them through the information that we can bring to them. It's their lives that are being talked about here. I think that, to me, and others in our studio, we really felt that we weren't able to reach that point, because we didn't spend enough time there; that's kind of the dilemma of this type of studio approach.

SL   But that also becomes an issue of familiarity, and this is where the idea comes in of setting up what could be almost a permanent institute, not necessarily in Chicago but perhaps in Boston, so there would be an area where Harvard was always working, so that there was a changing roster of students. It could be a partnership where the ideas and the exploration could be dealt with in a more comfortable way by both sides participating, where the community would know where these people stand. It would be an academic connection. But at the same time ideas could be shared. Pushing this studio idea to a higher level is one way of thinking about where this could progress.

EH   I think it would be a travesty if we dealt with this issue in a design bubble or in a planning bubble, to put a G-force around the GSD and not to have to deal with the residents or with the policy-makers.

CK There's no question in my mind that I got something out of this studio. It was not so much about how to design, but it was about definitely how to work, or how things work. The only hesitation I have is that, in the end, it was almost like you're experimenting on a group of people, without any real ability to do anything. People spend their whole lives doing what we set out to do in six months. The problems are too many and too vast to expect to be able to deliver something that they can use, something that's thoughtful. We can spend six years researching the place. I think it's crucial that these issues be talked about in places like the GSD. But I don't know that it's fair to the residents of a place like Stateway Gardens, or to the Merchants Association of 35th Street. They've been working on this for 15 years. It's a difficult line to walk.

DW What if the change did occur, though? They took the books that we produced from last semester and this semester and they're actually going through them now. They're picking out what they feel is relevant. So it's not whether you can go in and change anything, but what ideas you bring forth for them to think about.

CK They also have ideas. They first told us "we've got 15 plans on the shelf of how to do this. We don't have a dime, or we don't have the pull to pull it off." At a certain point, I think our objective always was to try and find a way to do this, and not just come up with a vision, which they clearly already have.

DW If Stateway Gardens was a vision too, at some level maybe you have to begin with a judgment amongst visions. Maybe it's fair to try and ascertain which vision is most appropriate. Not that we would necessarily be able to make that judgment but that's something that ostensibly, they in partnership with us, would be able to make.

People spend their whole lives doing what we set out to do in six months. The problems are too many and too vast to expect to be able to deliver...something that's thoughtful.

—CK

JB This all began with some vision, and maybe we can turn this conversation to a slightly different arena. In the context of all these planning issues and social issues, what design issues came up? And what role did design play in the studio, if any, and what came out?

BG There is a moment where we can begin to rephrase some of this discussion in a more positive light. In our studio, which was the first Bronzeville Studio, we began with a kind of fear of the accountability that we were faced with. We had to go and present several times, and we were afraid that people wouldn't understand our traditional mode of work. But at a certain moment we learned how to frame our ideas and our presentation. What we were coming with wasn't one vision, it was a series of little pieces. People in the studio began to become experimental about their work and toward the end of the term began trying different approaches with more intellectual freedom. Sam came up with a very interesting approach to the State Street Corridor planning, simply by beginning with a formal reading of the grid of Chicago. But it resulted in a planning proposal that he stood up and defended in front of planners and everyone—our final presentation was in front of 150 or 200 people at IIT. The majority of them were residents of the community that we were working in. It was very well received, this proposal, and yet it was very unexpected. It afforded him an opportunity to stand up with an experimental idea and to defend it in front of people who were faced with it as a real proposition.

RB Do you think that that's part of the nature of the studio—the fact that design and planning students in an interdisciplinary studio, are being forced to frame their products?

Integrating the smaller projects allowed people to stand freely, to develop a cluster of visions.

We tried to address both address both architectural and social problems, but I think that we operated kind of on the boundary of those two.

—**BG**

BG   We learned to talk about what it was that we were good at doing. Because our studio had less experience with planning, we realized that people can work better by kind of breaking the problem up into smaller projects, and then integrating them at the end. Integrating the smaller projects allowed people to stand freely, to develop a cluster of visions. We tried to address both architectural and social problems, but I think that we operated kind of on the boundary of those two.

BS   I think that we felt that we needed the support of other disciplines, and it would have helped to have Kennedy School students, law students; the whole kind of variety of students from other schools that could help. We weren't equipped to deal with policy issues, which was at least half of the problem. What we learned to do is to speculate about those things that we didn't know. But we also tried to tailor the problems to what we were good at, which to some extent was providing an architectural vision as well as a planning vision.

JB   Can anybody describe other design components of the studios?

EH   Well we're all pretty quiet, because we all realize that design took a back seat to some of the other issues. Our studio, Bronzeville II, had a similar sequence of events, where the beginning was kind of slow, we were treading on unfamiliar territory, and all of a sudden we had to be policy experts, we had to be education experts, which was actually very good. We could tie that back into our schemes. It wasn't until toward the end of the semester, that most of the groups came up with the main generator of their scheme. One group focused on co-generation. Another group focused on demographics and what kind of housing that would produce. A group also focused on education. But none of them were pure design projects first. They were always informed by issues that we thought were the most pressing.

CK   There were some good ideas in the end from our studio. The difficulty for me was that because all these other things were going on, there was very little criticism of the actual design work. So what was our strong point, that being design, ended up never really being challenged or critiqued in any way. A lot of the design part of it didn't get to the point that it could have.

DW   I know that Lee and Richard tried to be more critical of the design this semester.

BG   I think that resulted from our discussions at the end of the first studio.

RB   Was there any interaction between the fall and the spring?

EH   No, the only interaction was Derrick [the only participant in both studios].

RB   The studio did work in groups within the studio and with IIT, which is somewhat unusual. Does anyone want to comment on that?

DW   There was very little interaction with IIT except in the presentations in Chicago. But the group dynamic was interesting. I worked with Catherine Melina this past semester, and I told her three or four weeks ago for the final presentation that I felt as if I was married to her because we were spending so much time together.

CM   I want a divorce.

[Group laughter]

CK   Although there was no hierarchy. There wasn't someone who gets to make a decision instead of us all butting our heads together for six weeks.

BS   I would say the group dynamic part offered the same challenges as the project itself. Not having that hierarchy at the same time also leads the group to a very large degree of inefficiency, because you do a lot of infighting and arguing with each other. It's just a mess. When you're doing your own projects you at least always know what needs to be worked on or you develop your own rationale and priorities. In a group, it gets kind of confused. Like who's doing what, what should we be working on, and even then if something you're working on will be valid for the group. In the end, the group finally worked together and we were able to produce some decent work. But at the same time it was an incredibly painful process, kind of like going through adolescence.

RB   As I understand it, at the beginning of both studios each person did an individual presentation of his or her approach to design, and what s/he wanted to get out of the studio. There's been alot of talk about students in different disciplines working together. The question is: did students from the same disciplines find that there's a large variation of approaches, goals, desires?

the group dynamic part offered the same challenges as the project itself. Not having that heiarchy at the same time also leads the group to a very large degree of inefficiency.

—BS

GS   The fall studio was an urban design option studio, but eight of the 12 of us were architecture students. Going around the room that day, it was really the similarities that became apparent: we were all saying we wanted to work with public housing, to make a difference in some way. It was a conscious choice of quite a few people. Two-thirds of the studio took a studio outside of its discipline because of the subject of the studio. I think that's slightly different than second semester when it had the added weight of being the real estate development studio.

BG   In that studio, there was only one architecture student.

JB   What were the challenges for an architecture student in an urban design studio?

BG   I didn't really know what drawings to do, or what scale to draw at, or how much detail was required to adequately indicate a portion of a design. I asked myself questions like, "is massing okay, is a footprint okay? Do I need pavement patterns?" I had no idea, really, what constituted urban design as opposed to the design for a building. In that sense the studio was just an introduction. I felt that at the end, although we were a little green at dealing with urban design problems, in our studio it was to our advantage that we had less of an overarching vision for the whole area, and it became a more informal collection of larger than architectural projects—small-scale urban interventions or urban interventions that demarcated certain areas on the map. In the end our plan was more fragmentary and more capable of being implemented in parts, so we found an interesting middle ground between urban design and architecture.

STUDIO OPTIONS SPRING 1996

Existing High-Rise Towers Within New Urban Fabric

Douglas Manz MUP '96, Brent Stringfellow MArch '97, Gregory Taylor MAUD '97,
and André Vite MAUD '97, Perspective Views

Bronzeville II: The Revitalization of Stateway Gardens Public Housing

Leland D. Cott
Visiting Critic in Urban Planning and Design

Richard Graf
Visiting Critic in Urban Planning and Design

This year the department's Spring development studio concentrated on the revitalization and replacement of America's decaying urban public housing. The selected site was the Stateway Gardens Housing neighborhood on Chicago's South Side. As the second consecutive urban design and planning studio in the Bronzeville series, this was intended to be a creative investigation of the particular relationship between design and real estate economics for the renewal of large-scale public housing. The course integrated site analysis, programming, master planning, urban and architectural design with not-for-profit and for-profit market assessment and economic analysis. Alternative real estate finance models detailing varying levels of public and private participation were investigated. The studio was conducted in collaboration with the College of Architecture at the Illinois Institute of Technology. IIT and GSD students worked simultaneously on a similar design and real estate studio project and participated in neighborhood meetings and presentations.

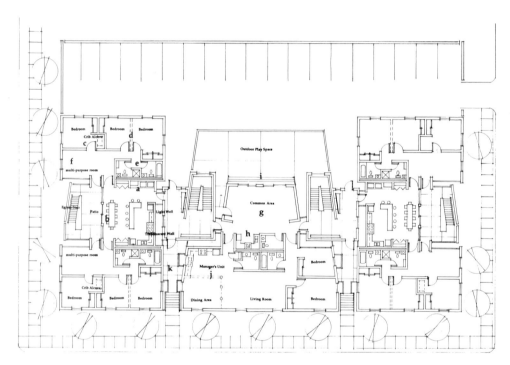

Lillian Kuri Maud '96 and Rachel Goldsmith MUP '96, Ground Floor Plan: Single Parent Housing

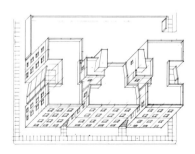

Axonometric View

Model View

Keith O'Connor MLAUD '96, Plans and
Sections Revealing Interaction of Natural
and Cultural Systems

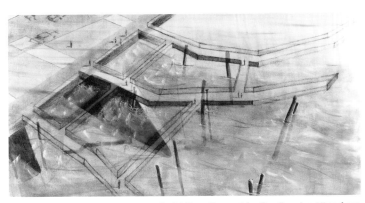

Aerial View: Proposal for San Francisco Waterfront

Embarcadero Open Space, Waterfront, and Transportation Project, San Francisco, CA

George Hargreaves
*Adjunct Professor of
Landscape Architecture*

Rebecca Krinke
*Visiting Critic in
Landscape Architecture*

This twenty-five-acre waterfront site in downtown San Francisco became available after the Loma Prieta earthquake rendered the freeway irreparable. What began as a marsh was transformed into a major transportation node where ferries and cable cars linked the Bay Area to San Francisco. In the 1960s the infamous Embarcadero freeway extension, with parking beneath it, became the dominant element of the waterfront.

The proposed program for the site's third transformation centered around open space elements such as festival and market plazas, green parks, waterfront promenades and transportation systems such as an on-grade arterial, bus termination zone, and trolley car extension. Studio participants were asked to propose a developed schematic design in media of their choosing. This was followed by complete design development of a system or moment for final review. There were several seminars with required readings and writing assignments that compared and contrasted precedents and situated the proposed project within a theoretical, critical, and historical context.

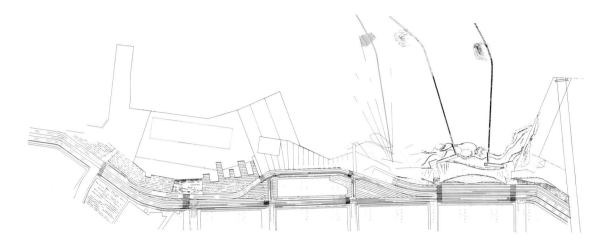

Site Plan from Market Street to the Bay Bridge

Clara Jimenez MLA '96, Topographic Plan

 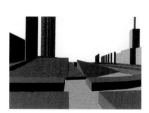 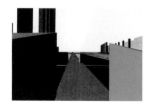 

Tae Wook Cha MLA '97, Sequential Experience of the Pedestrian Ferry Plaza

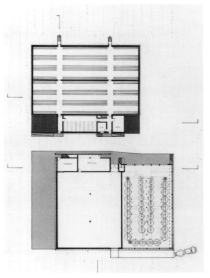

Plan

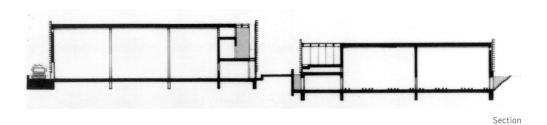

Section

Yuyang Liu MArch '97, Site Plan

A Winery in Yountville / Napa Valley

Jacques Herzog and
Pierre de Meuron
Arthur Rotch Design Critics in Architecture

The site was Napanook Vineyard in Yountville, one of the oldest vineyards in the Napa Valley. Napanook is a 124-acre estate where DOMINUS—one of the most prestigious Californian red wines— is produced. The vineyard is very gently sloped and offers spectacular views in all directions, namely to the famous Mount St. Helena, a former volcano in the north of the valley. The richness and variety of the soil is one of the reasons for the success of DOMINUS. Three different geological strata divide the vineyard in three different zones where the owner—a renowned French winemaker from Bordeaux— is cultivating different grapes: Cabernet Sauvignon, Cabernet Franc, Merlot, and Petit Verdot, according to the specific qualities of the site.

The project for a winery on the Napanook vineyard followed the brief for the construction of the DOMINUS winery, a project being realized by Herzog & de Meuron from 1995 to 1997. The program for the winery included a tank room, a barrel cellar, a warehouse with bottling facilities, some offices, and a tasting room.

Perspective View of the Barrel Cellar

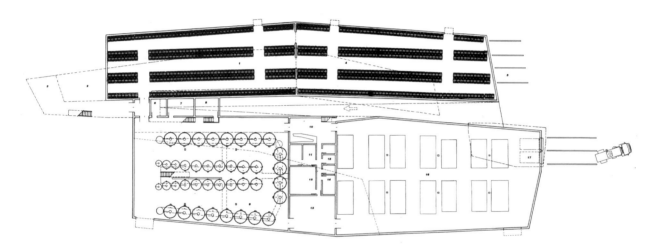

Ground Level Plan

 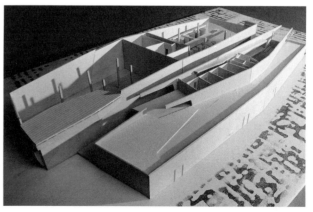

James Luhur MArch '98, Model Views

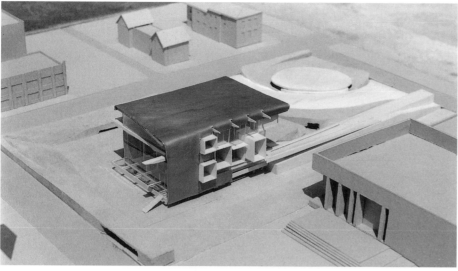

Model View From Southwest

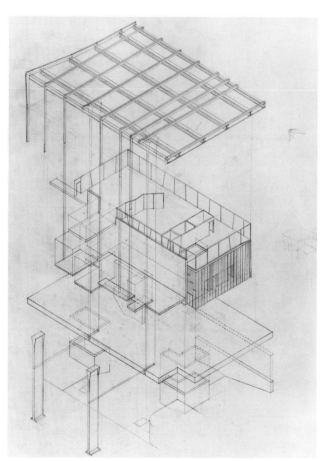

Isometric Study of Building Structure

An Information Center for Columbus, Indiana

Carlos Jimenez
Visiting Critic in Architecture

For more than half a century now, the small midwestern town of Columbus, Indiana, has been both celebrated and admired for its enlightened attitude toward architecture and its civic realm. Columbus also illustrates the impact that a singular corporation's patronage—through the generous vision of its founder—can impart on the making of the town itself.

The intent of this studio was twofold. One aspect involved the design of a 16,000 square foot Information Center to be located in downtown Columbus, within walking distance of Eliel Saarinen's much admired First Christian Church (1942). The building will function as a multipurpose visitor information center dedicated to the study of the town, its famed assemblage of buildings, and their common history.

The second concern throughout the duration of the studio entailed a critical discussion as to how architecture contributes to the life of the city—beyond the mere provision of objects to be consumed as museum pieces. Columbus offers both an element of resistance toward this tendency while at the same time nurturing it. The design of the Information Center was initiated by this dilemma and challenged by its broader implications.

A major emphasis was placed on the project's conceptual articulation(s) and its direct relationship to the building's construction and selection of materials. In addition to the given program, a courtyard/garden was to be included as a major design element within the site. The integration of landscape and public space as articulated in neighboring buildings designed by Saarinen, Roche, and Pei, among others, was carefully studied.

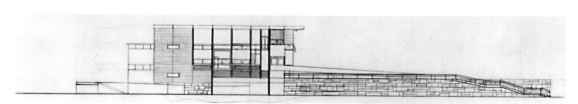

Andrew Liu MArch '97, Elevation of Information Center

David Bae MArch '97, Model View of Proposed Information Center

Approaches

The teaching of architecture today exposes students to a multitude of approaches as a consequence of our times' pervasive pluralism. Students confront these diverse possibilities and begin to gradually build their own approaches to architecture as they move from one studio to the next. The studio experience and the studio project are critical territories within which approaches are tested, validated, focused, and continued. Within this process, I believe teaching is ultimately a direct and exigent method—an exchange, actually—for guiding students to find their own approaches, and in turn contributing to their discovery of architecture.

I would like to focus on this exchange by commenting on the approach taken in my studio. The premise of the studio emanated from my firm belief that architecture must recapture its effectiveness in order to survive as a cultural force. Besides the widening disparity between theory and practice, one of the most troubling realities of architecture today is that its perception and message have been diluted by the primacy, indiscriminate production, and distribution of images. An immense void has emerged as architects surrender to the ephemerality of the image and the vanity of its projections. In a world that frequently mistakes velocity and novelty for progress, architecture must affirm its significance through the quietude of its emotive and material presence.I believe it is most urgent that students become aware of the impact that the work of architects can have on the lives of an individual, a community, and a city. Equally important is to discover what makes such work possible, and to understand the role of such work in the continuation of a culture.

The studio's project entailed the design of an information and visitor center for Columbus, Indiana, a small midwestern town known for a number of important works of architecture and an unusually enlightened attitude toward its civic realm. The site faced one of the town's most revered buildings, Eliel Saarinen's First Christian Church (1942). Rather than immediately commencing work on individual projects, students were asked to thoroughly examine the conceptual and physical qualities of any six outstanding buildings in the town. Two buildings, the Saarinen church and Robert Venturi's Fire Station Number 4 (1966) became particularly important in the students' exercises. Within the context of the project's intentions—by drawing, exploring, and visiting these buildings—students came to appreciate the clear resolution of the buildings' conceptual and material expression. The two buildings also illustrated quite succinctly the studio's objectives.

As students developed and formulated their approaches to the project, they faced the challenge of designing a tourist center in a town which, through its commitment to the patronage of architecture, has become a museum of buildings. The issue of tourism was stipulated as a neutral transaction within the town rather than as a malady of a consumptive public. The project posed a challenge not to create another building in isolation, on a pedestal, but to endeavor to produce an enriching public space by carefully integrating and structuring an architecture with its site.

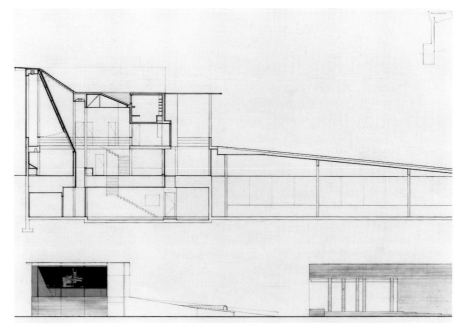

In coping with the multiplicity of approaches that students encounter in their education as architects, the one constant that must remain intact is their passion for the rigor of the discipline. Architecture is, more than anything else, the art of building. Herein lies its fortitude and its optimism.

Carlos Jimenez *was a Visiting Design Critic in Architecture during the 1995-96 academic year. His design office is based in Houston, Texas*

Longitudinal Section and Elevation

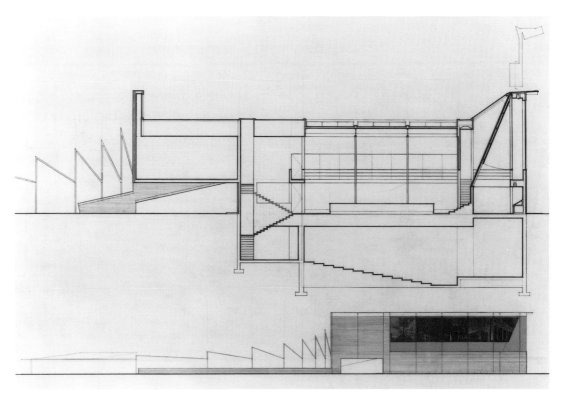

David Bae, Transverse Section and Elevation

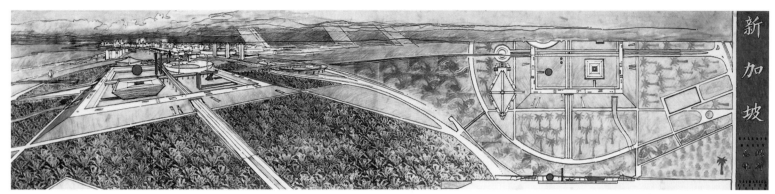

新
加
坡

Nathaniel Fuster Felix MAUD '96, Aerial Perspective View with Partial Plan and Section

Singapore Studio

Rodolfo Machado
*Professor in Practice of Architecture and
Urban Design*

This studio, kindly sponsored by the Urban Redevelopment Authority of Singapore, undertook the redevelopment of the Kallang Basin area. Located on the fringe of Singapore's Central Area, at the waters' edge, the site is traversed by two rivers and shows the results of the various land reclamation projects effected since 1930. The site includes the old Kallang Airport, the National and the indoor stadia as well as remarkable public housing buildings from the 1950s and 60s.

The program called for, essentially, 25,000 units of housing of various types and sizes, 88,000 square meters of commercial and recreational development plus those programmatic elements the students deemed essential for the production of an appropriate Singaporean urbanity.

The following points were of particular interest to the studio: first, the relationship between the notions of high density and normative urbanism; second, the relationship among "tropical architecture," interior architecture, and public space; and, third, the relationship between various "types" of democracy, cultural specificity, or the lack of it, and the built world.

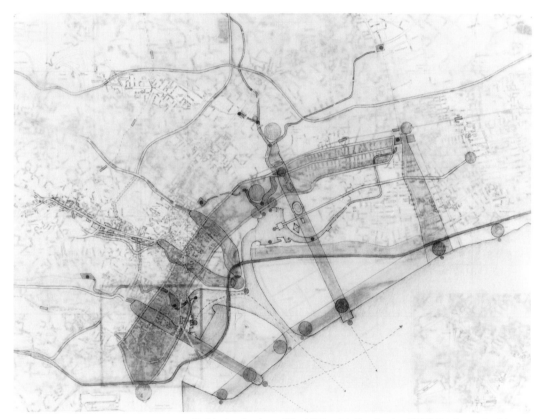

Christopher Broshears MArch '97 and Jeffrey Gordon MAUD '96, Generative Diagram

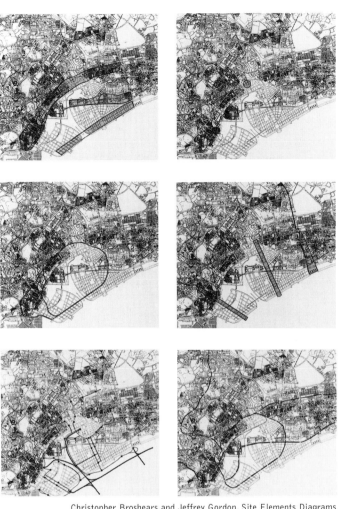

Christopher Broshears and Jeffrey Gordon, Site Elements Diagrams

Master Plan

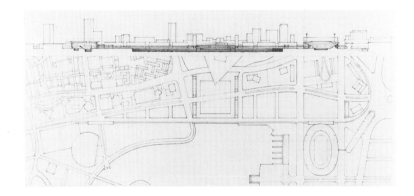

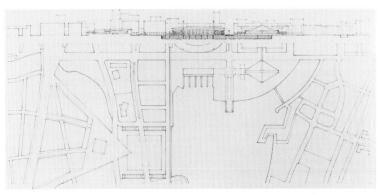

Plan/Sections of Kallang Basin
Looking North (top) and West (bottom)

The House and the City

Brian MacKay-Lyons
Visiting Critic in Architecture

If the house is the starting point of architecture, then the city or landscape is the ultimate architectural artifact. The house is the ground cover of the city, the connective tissue or fabric-making element.

Just as the urban or landscape context informs the design of the single infill house, in a proactive way, the design of a prototypical house embodies a latent urbanism. In other words, the house produces the form of the city. In this way, the house embodies at a grassroots level, the aspirations or pessimism of a people, a place, or an age. The Georgian terrace houses of Bath, England, the New England Cape Cod house, or Frank Lloyd Wright's Usonian house have all asserted powerful environmental design arguments within an Anglo-American context.

As we approach the third millennium, what is the zeitgeist or spirit-of-the-times? What optimism can the architecture profession project to regain its relevance in the eyes of society? If we have nothing to say about the house, then there is little hope for us as a profession.

Joshua Heitler MArch '97, Model Views

Model View

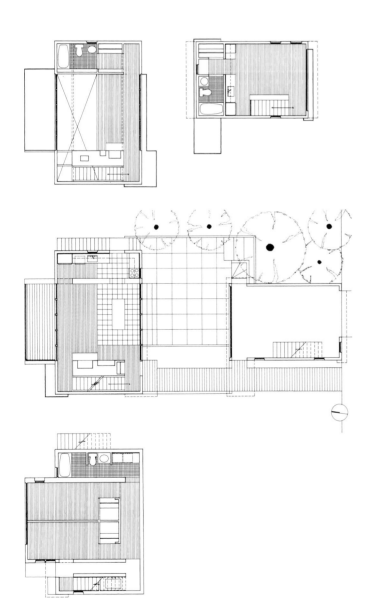

Plans

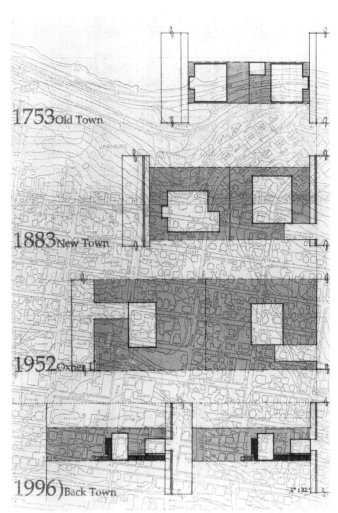

Lunenburg Settlement Diagram

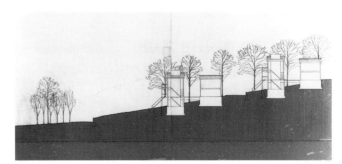

Gretchen Schneider MArch '97, Section Showing Relationships
of Houses to Each Other, Open Space, and Views

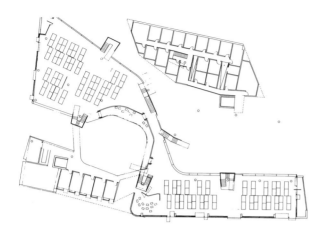
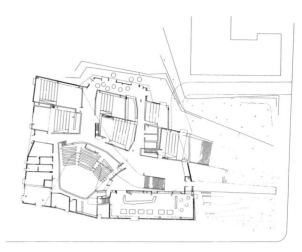

Plans: New Gund Hall

Another Quincy Street

Enric Miralles
Design Critic in Architecture

Scene 1. (Taxi at the airport. Clear sky. Cool, crisp morning.)

Taxi driver: "Mornin.' Where ya headin' pal?"

Passenger: "Quincy Street, Cambridge. On the double!"

ANOTHER QUINCY STREET.

Last year's studio worked under the title "one double, please" to learn from specific contemporary constructions. Students built a kind of pair. This repetition of the same program, site, etc., allowed the student to learn in this parallel between the existing building and their new proposed version.

This year's studio continued this line of work, but modified the condition of repetition. The subject of the exercise was Quincy Street, Cambridge. Each student took one of the buildings on the street and replaced it with a new Design School, Sackler Museum, Fogg Museum, etc., developing his or her project in the same place— once again "double, please!"

Each student project this year needed to be very aware of the proximity of its neighboring constructions. The projects paid maximum attention to the spaces between the buildings and the limits that define the way Quincy Street exists now.

This was an exercise in which the student needed to be aware of the very precise system of interior-exterior relationships that form the final construction of a street inside a campus. A complete model of the "new" Quincy Street, which included each student's project, was made at the end of the semester.

Andrew Burges MArch '96, Model Views of New Gund Hall

Model Views of New Emerson Hall

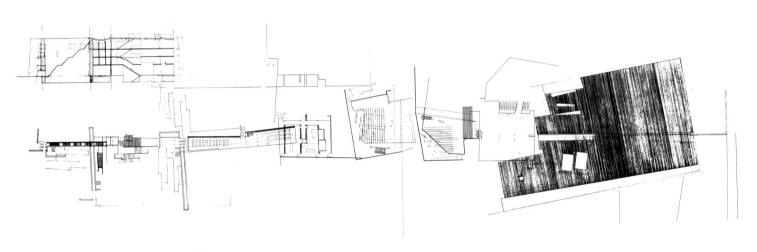

Continuous Plan/Section

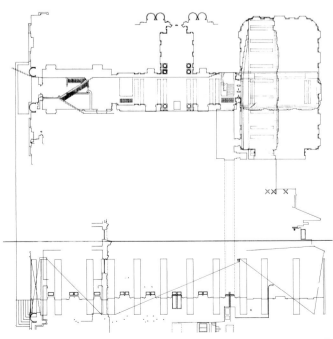

David Yocum MArch '97, Emerson Hall:
Transformation Drawing of Existing Building

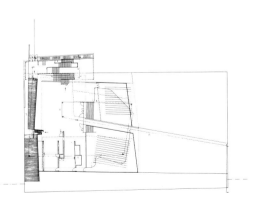

Plan: New Emerson Hall

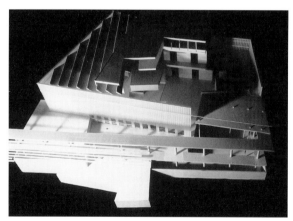

Model Views of New Fogg Art Museum Complex

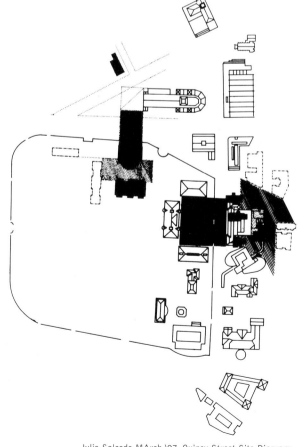

Julio Salcedo MArch '97, Quincy Street Site Diagram,
Showing Displacement of Memorial Hall

Model View

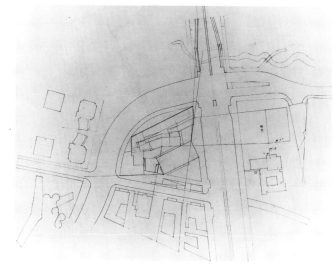

Site Plan

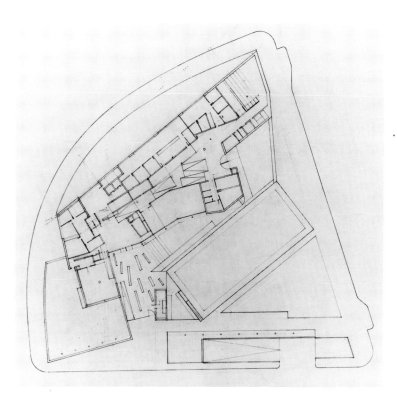

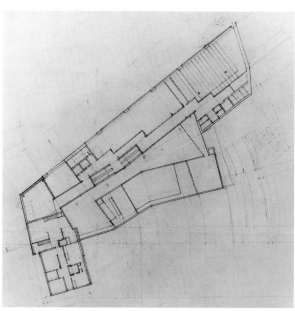

Andrew Davis MArch '96, Plans

An American Embassy in Berlin

José Rafael Moneo
Josep Lluis Sert Professor of Architecture

Berlin is today the city with the strongest building activity in the world. To recreate the conditions of a capital metropolis that was literally destroyed in the war, and that subsequently suffered such an awkward partition, is one of the most intriguing planning problems that an architecture student can approach. The development of proposals that address these complex problems became an important part of the theoretical substance developed in the studio's work.

The studio focused on a specific problem, the project for an American Embassy in the new German capital. In their designs for the building, students needed to consider the following issues: recognition of the site conditions, programmatic resolution, and the representation of German history with all its ideological implications.

The proposed building is a complex that houses the new embassy, its administration, consulate, cultural services, and ambassador's residence. The elaboration of the complex forced students to consider the issue of architectural language as it emerges with all its potency.

Students began by analyzing Berlin as a whole and quickly focused on an actual site, a parcel of land along the Tiergarten where the Nordic embassies complex will actually be located. Ultimately, we compared our results with those of the recently projected American Embassy in Berlin.

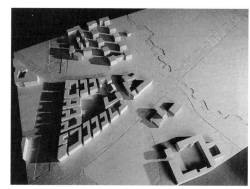

Site Model

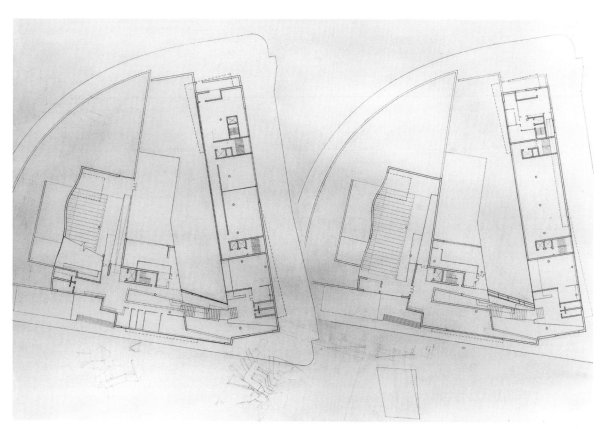

Plans

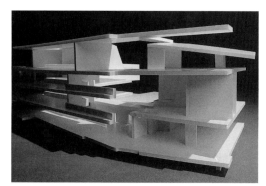

Model View

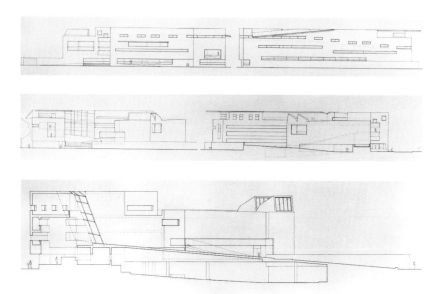

Brian Bell MArch '97, Elevations and Section

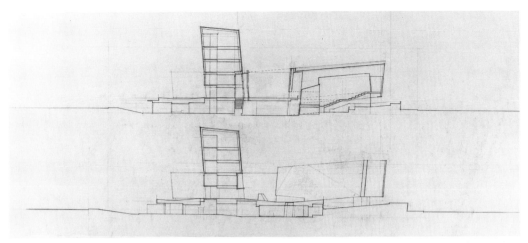

Longitudinal Sections

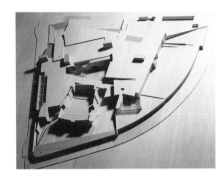

Model Views

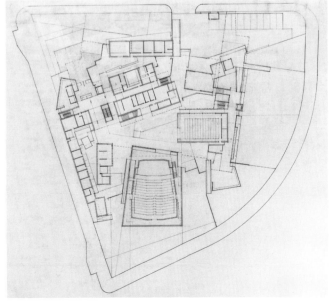

Yu-Han Michael Lin MArch '97, Ground Floor Plan

Aerial Photomontage of Site

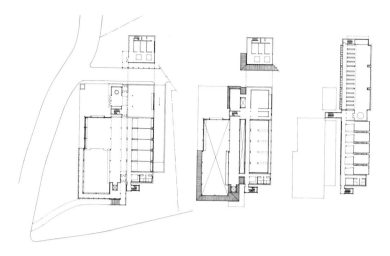

Robert Winstead MArch '97, Plans

Education and Fabrication: Master Plan for Artisans' College

Toshiko Mori
Professor in Practice of Architecture

In a small coastal New England town, there exists a newly established college for undergraduate studies based on philosophy, history, and the tradition of the boat building technology. The current enrollment is between 35 and 40 and the curriculum is centered around the crafting and building of boats and vessels. The college is re-establishing its mission and is seeking a new vision in order to expand its currently limited application in our time. The questions are: Is boat building becoming an obsolete profession, as the whaling industry became in New England? Are they building a precious piece of an exquisite instrument to be thrown into the water? What is its future and will it survive a shift of mode to computer-aided fabrication? What will the graduates of this college be able to contribute to our society at large? While the act of fabrication by hand and by machine can enhance the understanding of the making of our environment, it faces the inevitable transition between manufacturing and automated fabrication. The comparative value judgment of handmade pieces, machine-made pieces, and computer-simulated pieces was a central question of this studio's investigation.

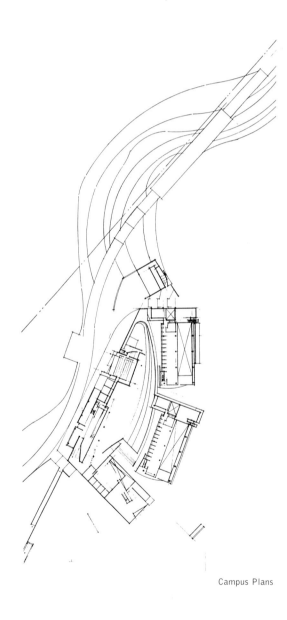

Campus Plans

Karin Tehve MArch '97, Housing Study:
Aggregation of Dwellings

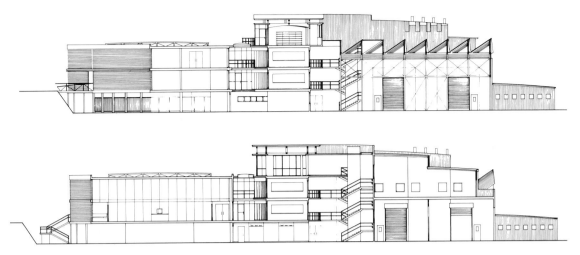

Transverse Sections

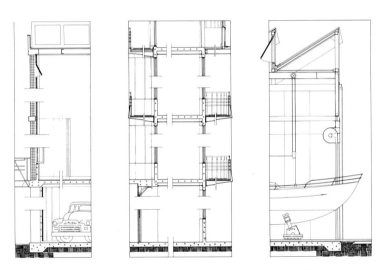

Sectional Details

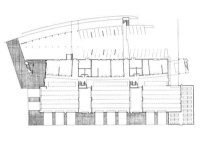

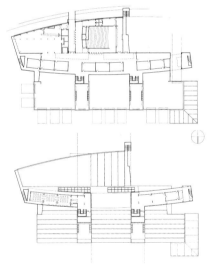

Plans

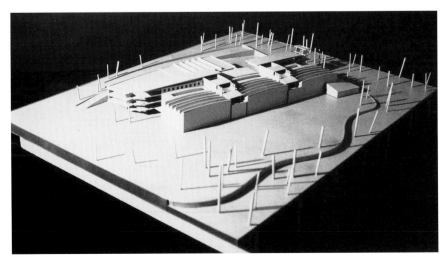

David Curtin MArch '97, Model View

Detail of Plan

Inten(c)ity on the Flats

Dennis Pieprz and Steven R. Krog
Visiting Critics in Landscape Architecture and Urban Design

Located in an oxbow of the Cuyahoga River, the Scranton Road Peninsula is a 64-acre parcel of industrially impacted land in "The Flats," which lies tantalizingly close to the Central Business District of Cleveland, Ohio. Students were asked to address questions of (1) the nature of the urban experience and (2) how the design of the project site could support and enhance that experience in light of the fact that, although physically close to the city, the site is isolated by the moat-like effect of its river boundary. Not a suburb and, yet, not quite a part of the downtown, the Peninsula is ripe for a new generation of use(s). Students first programmed those uses and then carried selected aspects of the proposal to a level of detailed design development.

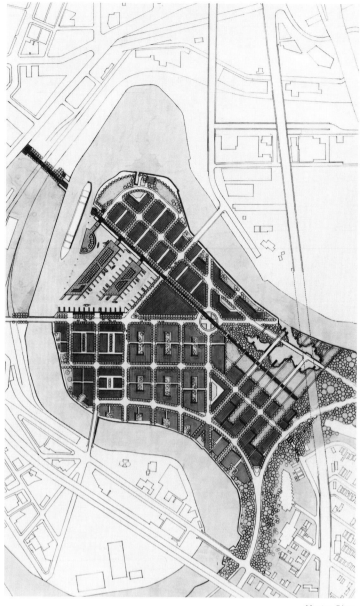

Master Plan

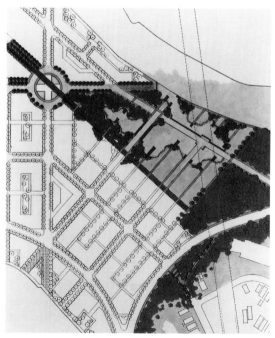

Sherman Stave MLA '97, Detail of Plan

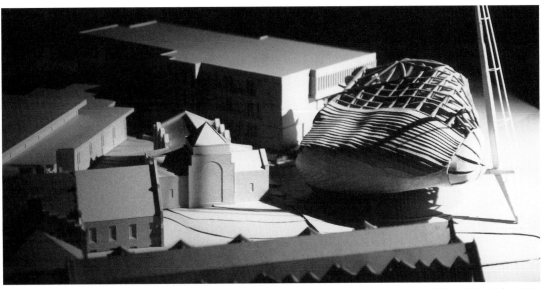

Aerial View of Model from West

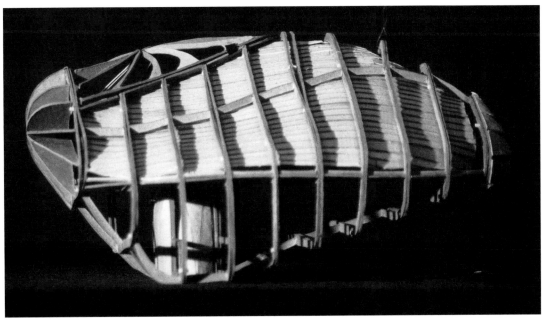

Alan Christ MArch '97, Model View: North Elevation

Untitled 6

Chris Risher, Jr.
Design Critic in Architecture

The aim of this studio was to coax figures to emerge in architectural form. We carefully observed a lovely existing early Christian Basilica on Memorial Drive in Cambridge (the Monastery Chapel of the Society of Saint John the Baptist). As a studio we made careful watercolor paintings of the existing building through the term, while from the first day we designed a chapel of identical functional requirements to replace the existing building on the existing site.

We read the late work of Ludwig Wittgenstein as a cautionary tale of liberation from certain obligations to the field of experience in favor of a ground on which shy figures play and have played well before 20th-century conceits embarrassed them and made them hide.

This studio was not preoccupied with historical obligation; neither was it designed to promote cause and effect connections between program and building. It did, however, accept the use to which the Chapel is put today, and the place where it stands as a binding set of limits regarding the proposal for its replacement.

Ana Sotrel MArch '97, Light Studies

Shape

School likes things that can be known. So does the twentieth century. We like knowing better than being. We take comfort in structure but we're fearful of shape. Shape is too mysterious, and so is being. They're both indulgent. We play it safe: we go for structure and give the other two a handicap.

Structure promises architects and critics an adventure where the unknown is stalked by the known—in which what is yet to be known is a secular grail. The strengths and physics of things—our use and appreciation for them—search in a vanished ontological state, like Mississippi. As if in Cervantes, knowing and structure look for being and shape.

A saw has it that engineers know little about art. They substitute efficiency for beauty. It is harder for us to admit that architects know little about shape. We dote on structure and shame profile. We filigree edge and scatter silhouette. We are Victorians with a mission. Like engineers who see truth in efficiency, we see beauty in the contraction of space as time.

Time is to structure as shape is to space. Time knows no boundaries, but shape does. To differentiate a thing is to model structure as a distribution in time. Our mission is to decorate space with these models and march them through walls as if they were time itself. Time marches through walls leaving space intact. But when we order space to march through walls, both are gone.

Structure can be prophetic in design work no less than efficiency, but it is false in its prophecy of form. It is false when it subordinates shape to service itself. In defining form, the dictionary joins shape and structure with a coordinating conjunction. Indeed, if order is of consequence in the layout of meaning, it should be noted that in Webster's shape comes before structure.

When we pursue form, it would seem that we should permit neither shape nor structure to take authority; neither should rule the other. Neither should be a by-product. If they come together in the end, they should be tended to separately along the way: as in a famous Afghani rice and spinach dish, the two primary ingredients must be prepared in different ways before being put together in the final cooking.

Standing precariously on the I-55 Frontage Road in Jackson, I turn 360 degrees. Everywhere I see structure. Everywhere I see twentieth-century profligacy in structure—road signs and circulation, zoning and property patterns, cars and lots, poles and lines. Colors are fixed in figure-ground targets. Market force and structure authorize shape to dispatch an army of ground troops in camouflage gear. But why should I be surprised? When I see schoolwork and so much hard-fought practice, it is all the same. Why should school be different. The schools lead world makers; they lead where they've been led—and earlier in this century they were led away from shape.

Once students loved the shapes of things. They came to school seeing the world as shapes. But teachers demanded that students put shape away. Look at how things are made, they said. Look at colors and patterns; see the weight, size, and texture of things. Those teachers were not tyrants. More than anything, they wanted students to feel and see anew. It is true that they worried about a world overrun with authoritarian shapeliness, an agent of concealment regarding important political, social, and technical structure. But more than that, they wanted to surprise students by showing them aspects of the world long hidden. They used shock to open eyes. Over the years, teachers have continued with what once gave a start. Ironically enough, over those same years, their advocacies—fused with economic, intellectual, and literary initiatives—succeeded in remaking the world to fit their schoolhouse studies.

What is more, surprise is lost to our students. Need one say that structure is ubiquitous? Students arrive in school attracted to structure as once they were to shape. Structure is the a priori exhibit and exegesis of second nature as it is constructed today.

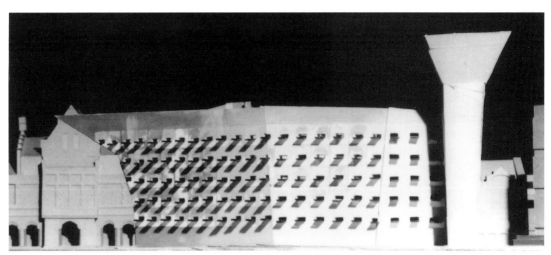

Francis Howarth MArch '97, Model View

It is ironic that many would-be modernists substitute structure for shape and thus for form. If the first order of form is authority, within that order we find many propositions, at least two of which have to do with shape. First, as distinct from content, form can be known from the outside. Second, like an egg in hand, form shows many possibilities and uses. And however much that choice is constrained, constraint itself, like its absence, is a show of choice in the action of authority. But while such authority can be put to good or to evil purpose, it is important to remember that denial of access to the interior of form does not entirely deny access to the nature of that condition. In this sense, form put to most uses is more liberating than content. And shapely form—one might say true form—is more liberating than structure purporting to be form. The contrary prison of structure as shape reconstructs content to be structure. Making glib substitutions, architects attack the authority of witness by confusing certain distinctions, foremost among them contrast between inside and out. Without such distinctions, authority ceases to protect freedom of witness.

The validation of form is abstract. It does not permit an interchange of form and content. But without shape and the maintenance of space therein, form can be confused with type. Properly shaped and thus defended, space makes room to move. It becomes a large house for many functions. Co-opted by a vision of architecture in which functions of time replace shape, room to move, or form, is replaced with moments of fusion between what would be form and content, an enormous family of little types.

Chris Risher, Jr. *was Design Critic in Architecture during the 1995–96 academic year.*
His architecture practice is based in Jackson, Mississippi.

Simon Gathercole, Cambridge Exchange,
Model View: Interior

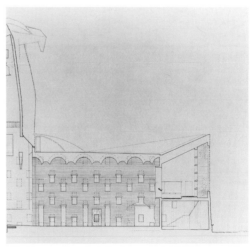

Section: Looking South

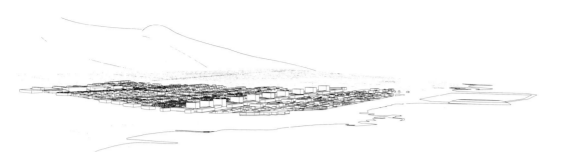

Thomas Doxiadis MArch/MLA '98, Aerial Perspective

Isopolis: Addressing Scales of Urban Life in Athens

Peter Rowe
Raymond Garbe Professor of Architecture and Urban Design
Dean, Faculty of Design

Hashim Sarkis
Design Critic in Architecture

The studio addressed the general question of how large tracts within a metropolitan area, formerly the site of major infrastructure improvements, can be redeveloped to productively address different scales of urban life. With changes in transportation technology, as well as ways and means of producing goods and services, many cities now have well-located and otherwise valuable parcels of land potentially available for development. The question was how can this redevelopment take place in a socially and environmentally beneficial manner?

The site for this studio investigation was the existing airport in Athens, Greece, following the proposed relocation of the airport function to the east of the city. Currently, the airport is located relatively close to the center of Athens, parallel to and close by the sea. Areas to the north and south of the existing airport are well established and likely to continue to be valuable sites for residential as well as commercial development. Transit improvements to this part of the city have been planned—vastly improving potential overall access—and the area seems likely to receive considerable attention as the site for major recreational and leisure-time facilities.

The three scales addressed in the studio, through both program and site development, were national/regional, metropolitan, and local. Moreover, it was clear that any proposal for the existing airport site must operate well at all three scales in order to be both socially successful and politically acceptable to the Athens community. This problem was further complicated by the presence of several municipal jurisdictions covering the site.

The studio was partially sponsored by the Harvard Hellenic Foundation, allowing students to make a site visit to Athens.

Detail Plan

Nancy Conger MLAUD '96, Site Plan

Perspective Rendering Looking Toward Waterfront

Nicholas Stanos MAUD '96, Site Plan

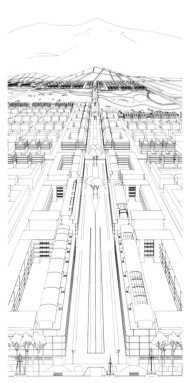

Thomas Rammin MAUD '97, Site Plan

Perspective View

Site Plan

Lital Szmuk MLA '96, Perspective Photomontage

Art and Surface Mine Reclamation

Martha Schwartz
Adjunct Professor of Landscape Architecture

This studio explored the landscape as an artistic medium. The student's formal solution to the problem depended on the clarity of that student's personal aesthetic agenda and his/her ability to express these ideas/sensibilities through the manipulation of the land.

The aim of the studio was to demonstrate that selected mines can, through the inclusion of design in the reclamation process, offer substantial social, cultural, and aesthetic amenities to the public at costs equal to or below the standard costs of reclamation. The means of achieving this objective were to redesign a selected open pit mining site from those that have been geophysically reclaimed in fulfillment of the Surface Mining Control and Reclamation Act (SMCRA) of 1977, and regulations 30 CFR Part 700. The redesigned landscapes will offer, in addition to meeting required environmental standards, "cultural landscapes" incorporating user amenities whose economic, social, and aesthetic features can be benchmarked, for value comparisons, against similar design features in comparable locations.

The issue at hand was not whether reclamation should be done, but how it is to be done. The standard requirements for this process, although "ecologically"

sound, are often accomplished in visually substandard ways: mining companies may fulfill reclamation regulations, yet the end results are often unsightly, awkward, and under-utilized. These "reclaimed landscapes" often remain isolated from their adjacent landscapes and are visual eyesores. The continued visual poverty of these landscapes also discourages reuse or reintegration of the land for social uses.

The thesis of this studio was that the goals of the reclamation process should be broadened to include a visual component so that despoiled landscapes can once again be useful to society.

The legal requirements and guidelines for the reclamation process are quantitative in nature. They spell out a specific number of trees per square foot, angle of slope, minimum areas of ground cover, water treatment standards, etc. Because of the difficulty in setting visual standards or a general lack of expectation for reclaimed sites by the public, almost all reclamation is done through engineering forms where there are relatively few professionals who focus on visual or qualitative issues. The reclamation process is focused on the quantitative issues of repair or the technical aspects of rebalancing a natural ecology, but holds no requirements that these repairs be done so that the result is a visually attractive or sympathetic landscape. The results of most reclamation efforts, whether they be the capping of landfills or regrading and planting of abandoned mines, is mundane and perfunctory. Most

James Lord MAUD '96, Plan

often, these sites remain strange and awkward lumps, veneered with a thick skin of grass. Transformed to a degree, they remain visual and cultural wastelands.

The studio attempted to illustrate that when a reclamation process includes a strong "design component," the resulting product will have additional value and potential for future use, beyond that which results from our present set of standards. We wanted to make the case for the inclusion of new requirements that include landscape architects and artists in the existing reclamation process. This is the missing step in site reclamation if that site is ever to function as part of our cultural landscape.

Section

Model Views

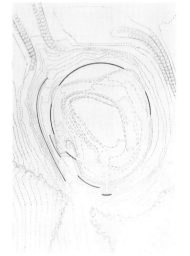

Partial Plan

Jennifer Brooke MLA '96, Partial Plan

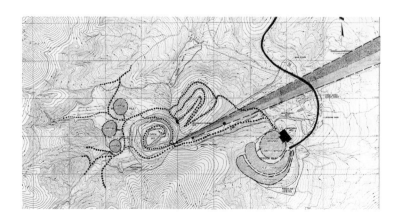

Christian Lemon MLA '97, Site Plan and Section

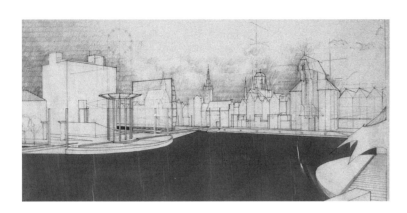

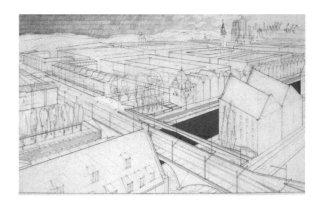

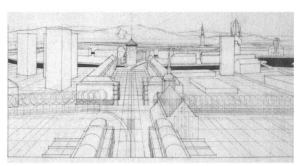

Perspective Views of Linear Interventions

Strategic Urban Redevelopment in Gdansk, Poland

Mona Serageldin
Adjunct Professor of Urban Planning

David Neilson
*Visiting Critic in Urban Planning
and Design*

This is one of a series of studios on urban issues in societies undergoing economic restructuring, institutional transformation, and social change. The pedagogic interest of these studios, prepared by the GSD Unit for Housing and Urbanization, is to allow urban planners and designers interested in working in diverse economic and social settings to develop the sensitivity and skills required to devise strategies meeting the challenge of rapid and profound transformation and to shape culturally adapted responses to the needs of changing societies.

The studio explored strategies for urban development for Gdansk that capitalize on the strengths of the various networks of cities in which it is an active participant. Such an approach to planning and urban design suggests the simultaneous use of a multiplicity of actions at different scales related to different time horizons.

The studio focused on the under-used land adjacent to the city's port area which includes Granary Island directly across from the historic Old Town. This sector is a critical node linking the city's diverse districts on the upper and lower banks of the Motlawa River. The redevelopment of this strategic site will shape the city's future urban structure.

Looking to the city's 1000th anniversary in 1997, the studio developed visions for Gdansk in the first decade of the 21st century related to the strategies designed to strengthen its position within the European Union and the Baltic Sea Region.

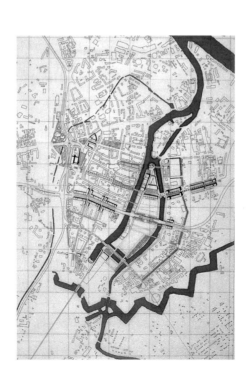

David Gamble MAUD '97, Plan: Linear Interventions

Alicia Guajardo MUP '97,
Proposed Transportation Lines

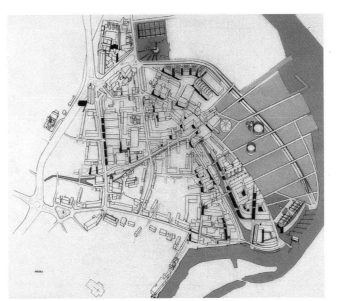

Plan: Expansion Areas

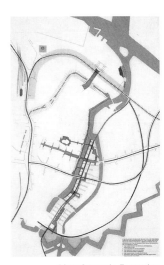

Plan: Strategic Expansion

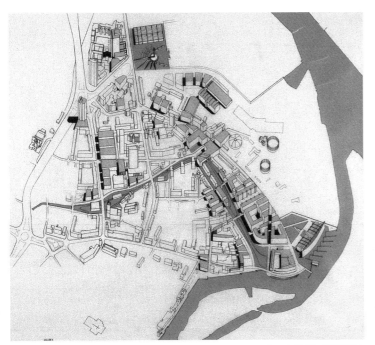

Sameh Wahba MUP '97,
Plan: Development Areas

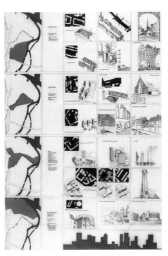

Urban Fabric Analysis

Photomontage: Rotary Site

Model View: Rotary Site

Relics, Prosthetics, and Surrogate Space

Ken Smith
Visiting Critic in Landscape Architecture

Infrastructure has supplanted nature as the dominant pre-condition in determining urban space. This studio explored the culture and nature of infrastructure in shaping new urban environments. The new landscape implied by this concept is composed of relics, prosthetics, and surrogates of culture and nature. Replicants and simulations constitute a synthetic reality in which new landscape is space recaptured or re-deployed from within the context of existing urban structure.

This studio looked at two types of sites, both in New York City, but representative of types existing in all urban areas. One type of site involved assembling bits and pieces of leftover landscape into something usable and viable as landscape form. The vehicular approaches to the Holland Tunnel and the Canal

Street connections are one such site, a landscape opportunity in the context of a tough environment and complicated pedestrian and traffic patterns. Another type of site involved large-use areas with a complicated program and large-scale landscape use patterns. JFK Airport is such a site, with potential for expressive landscape design, either at a site-specific intervention level or at a larger scale of establishing new landscape framework. Both types of sites have landscape opportunities that are unseen and unrealized but viable areas for landscape architectural inquiry and design. These sites are pedagogically useful since the context forces landscape conceptualization in non-traditional terms and development of fresh design forms.

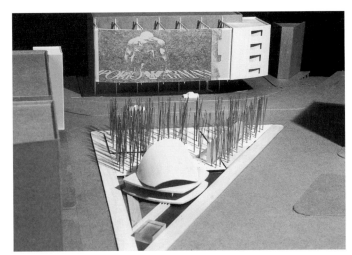

Gerdo Aquino MLA '96, Model View: A Small Park, Screen, and Apartments

Felice Grodin MArch '97, Model View: Entrance to the Holland Tunnel

Perspective View Along Waterfront

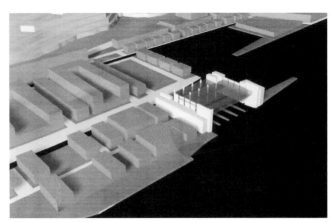

Aerial View of Terminal

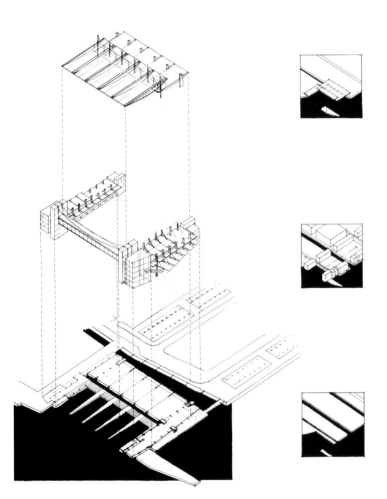

John Adams MAUD '96, Exploded Axonometric and Diagrams

Ferries on the Hudson: Urban Architecture and Infrastructure

Marilyn Jordan Taylor
and David M. Childs
*Visiting Critics in Urban Planning
and Design*

As New York City faces the challenge of enhancing and extending its critical transportation systems, a serious question of scarce resources arises. One quick and valid response is the reintroduction of the ferries that served the city in previous decades but were largely discarded with the proliferation of cars and buses. Today's ferries are different, though: quicker, smaller, lighter, they can move surprising numbers of commuters, shoppers, theatergoers, and tourists in a flexible, efficient, and pleasant trip across and along the Hudson and around other New York waterways. Like other systems of urban transportation, they offer the potential for organizing pedestrian-related communities around their terminal sites.

This studio explored in sequence the architectural and urban design potential of three urban locations along the Hudson River where ferry service, new or expanding, will have a considerable and profound effect on the communities and riders it serves. At each location the form and image of the ferry terminal was studied in relationship to the design of new adjoining development. These three locations included a New Jersey riverfront site with significant development potential, a Battery Park City site integrally tied to the new commodities exchange, and an Upper West Side site with tourist and recreational potential involving the reuse of an existing landmark structure.

The first challenge was to create a visual presence and identity for the ferry, to speed riders on their trip while also celebrating the ride; the second challenge was to use the investment in terminals to stimulate new districts and communities that will serve New York City and the Hudson River communities as they enter the 21st century.

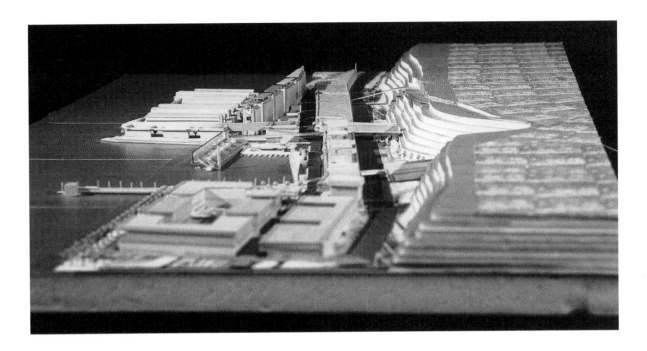

Steven Stainbrook MAUD '97, Model Views

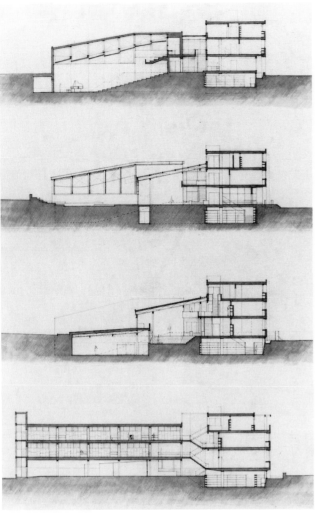

East-West Sections

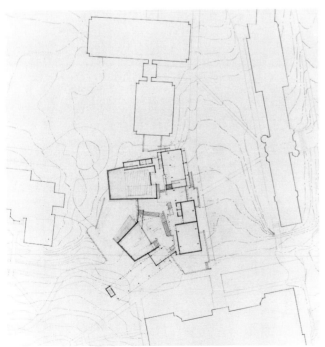

Lisa Huang MArch '97, Site Plan

Perspective View

A New Building for the Department of Music at Princeton University

Rafael Viñoly
Kenzo Tange Visiting Critic in Architecture

Music has been compared—often in a rather simplistic fashion—with architecture for many different reasons, especially in regard to the relationship between its abstract dimension and the ways in which it operates through very concrete means of expression.

Although music and architecture are extremely diverse fields (both as practices as well as aesthetic endeavors), there are some interesting parallels between them that are useful to explore, such as, the similarities in their approach to the use of compositional techniques, and curiously enough, the significant differences in the ways in which they are taught.

The design problem of this course (a relatively uncomplicated building program) enabled us to focus on two issues, which seem to have been systematically postponed in recent years of architectural training: the relationship among invention, virtuosity, and performance, and the significance of the non-visual aspects of architectural work.

The Princeton campus is a special environment where the problem of stylistic consistency and the inevitability of formal innovation is not only a critical design subject but also one that is at the center of an open intellectual debate. The program of the building is composed of a variety of cellular and assembly spaces, of different environmental characters and very specific acoustic and structural requirements that conform a rather unconventional architectural material.

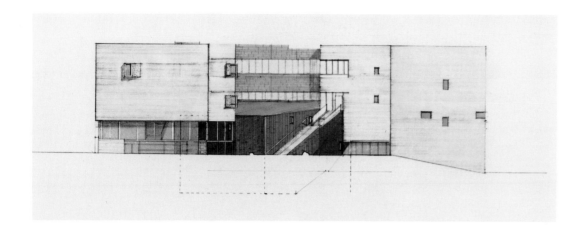

Elevations

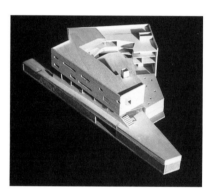

Model View

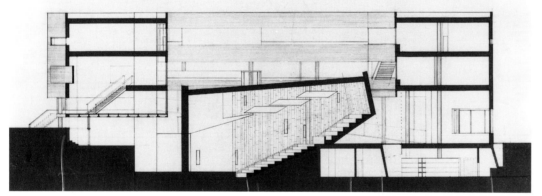

Section

Abigail Turin MArch '97, Site Plan

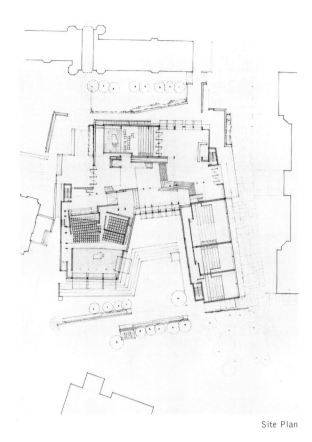

Site Plan

Model View

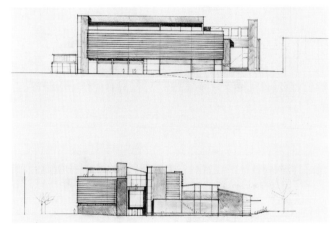

North and East Elevations

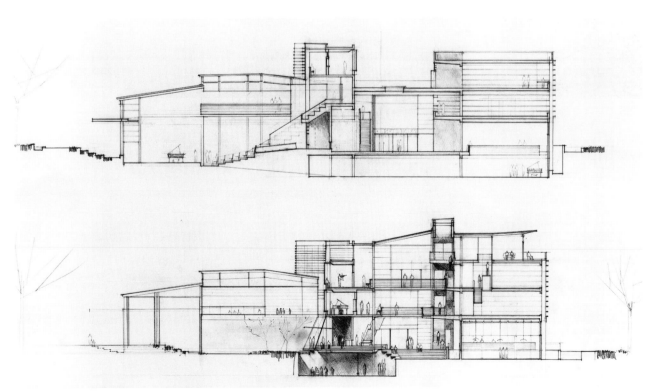

Amy Lin MArch '97, Sections Through Theater and Courtyard

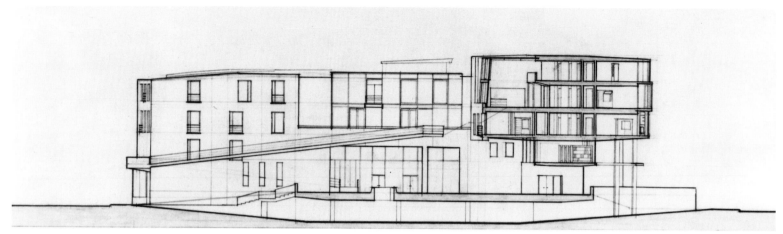

Section

Life Cycles IV:
Making Do With Less

Wilfried Wang
Design Critic in Architecture

The pursuit of happiness is an enshrined value not only of the Constitution of the United States of America, but it is the very core value of the American dream. Yet the gap between real happiness, true comfort, and its virtual representations has been growing since the 1960s. Architecture has, in this respect, proven to be the willing handmaiden of masking this gap, even though there have been numerous genuine attempts at bridging it.

The first task of the studio was to represent the difference between values pursued and values attained. Simple analyses were undertaken to come to such understandings.

The second task was to see which approaches for negotiating such a difference are tenable. These approaches might initially relate to the subject of the analyses of the first exercise or might relate to the specific paradigmatic assignment of investigating whether it is desirable and/or possible to design an environment for old people.

Old people's life-styles as a paradigm for making do with less...

In most post-industrial societies, about three out of one hundred families consist of three generations. Eight out of ten individuals die in hospitals. Thus, environments for old people are both the undiscussed norm as well as a growing sector in the provision of health care. The studio investigated whether this is indeed an unavoidable norm, or whether this norm can be challenged. Most people who grow old tend to make do with less, either as a matter of choice or as a matter of circumstances beyond their control. The studio drew lessons from such changed circumstances to see whether making do with less is a paradigm for post-industrialized societies as a whole.

Designing the environment

Whatever approach was chosen, the studio investigated such environments from the most proximate detail to the larger, invisible "structure," including the abstract organizational framework within which "making do with less" might become possible.

Erik Ajemian MArch '97, Model Views

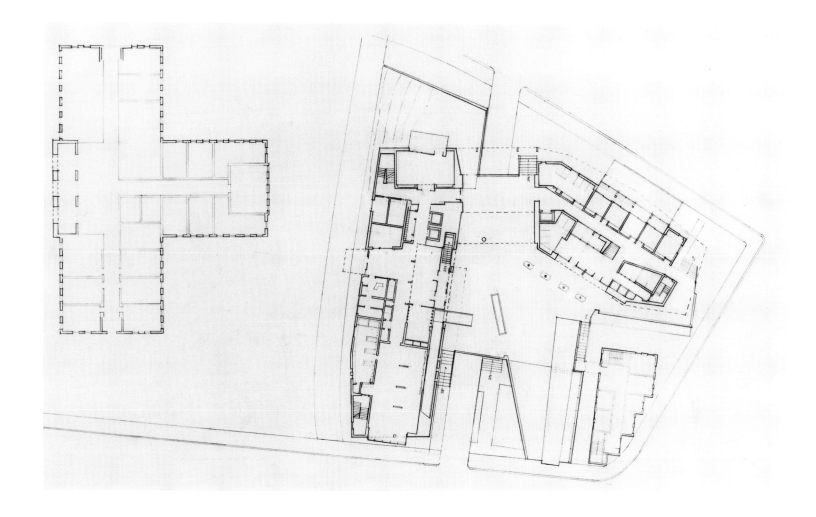

Eric Ajemian, Plans

From Style to Self-critical Sensibilities

Some years ago, the model of master classes was discussed in relation to the large, almost factory-like methods of continental European schools of architecture. The manner in which the Architectural Association School of Architecture (in London) conducted its education under the chairmanship of Alvin Boyarsky was emulated across England, and later gained favor in a number of continental European institutions.

The tendency was clear: successful teachers were identified on the basis of their power to groom acolytes; the closer the master's style was reproduced by the students, the better. Large continental European schools could only achieve this through osmosis via teaching assistants, who were more or less party-liners, seeing to it that students themselves would fall into line.

Boguslaw Trondowski MArch '97, Plan and Axonometric Analysis of Pattern Book Homes

Weakness in pedagogy was thus seen in those studios. A variety of designs were produced: seen from afar, the different designs seemed to lack coherence. Taken together, all the studios in a school would, in turn, be seen in rather superficial stylistic terms. There was a tendency to look for a style that would represent a school, or to identify the omnipresence of a single mind that could set the imprimatur, in both senses of the word, on the collective work.

When the AA model came to the United States in the 1980s, some "strong" schools already existed with more or less clearly associated in-house styles. The Graduate School of Design at Harvard, so Klaus Herdeg argued, gave rise to the 'decorated diagram;' Cornell under Colin Rowe fused Le Corbusier's syntax with the pleasures of poché; MIT staunchly defended Frank Lloyd Wright's 'passing connections' until they could be safely revisited with Neo-Constructivism, and so on.

Of course, students with a particular set of design skills developed their own fields of interest, despite school orthodoxies. Yet the structure and reliance, and in some cases insistence, on the notion of style as a mark of intellectual quality, has survived from the Hegelian era, and it survives to this day. Art and architectural history are still taught with stylistic categories in mind; stylistic thinking still appeals to teachers and students alike. The new style for the epoch, the genius architect who invents a new style, and originality, are concepts with continuing currency. To my mind, adherence to these notions indicates a fundamental insecurity about place: the specificities of time, site, task, and designer are neglected by this sense of insecurity. One of the most important aspects of the thesis project at the GSD is the inevitable particularity of research and therefore the differences of its outcome. Theses ask students to develop a particular approach and it seems that most rise to the occasion. Option studios can have a preparatory role. On the one hand, there can be a common question revolving around a single site, theme, or even program, but the requirements of specific developments require students to lay their own ground in a manner similar to proposing a thesis.

Take the theme of 'doing more with less,' for example. Applying it to the question of residences for an aging society, elicits a whole range of solutions, depending on individual questions and approaches. Differences that emerge are about larger social and cultural questions, which must be consciously asked and somehow resolved. Whether one believes in reforming the conventional approach to elderly housing or whether one attempts to design a residential unit capable of changing in size, allowing different configurations for changing needs over time, the exercise requires at the outset certain assumptions about patterns of life that go beyond the more autonomous formal and spatial possibilities of architecture.

An option studio can thus be seen as a link between the exploratory ground work necessary for architectural articulation in the core years and the unique research required of the thesis. None of these studio pedagogies need be oriented toward master classes as, I believe, we do not need the concentration of quality in a few memorable stars. To the contrary, we require the widest possible diffusion of the honest, self-critical questions that can be asked by individuals capable of consciously and continuously striving for the highest quality in their designs. Perhaps this is studio pedagogy's most important gift: self-critical sensibility as intellectual sustenance for the long and, often, barren road of real practice.

Wilfred Wang, *Director of the German Architecture Museum in Frankfurt, is a Design Critic in Architecture at the GSD.*

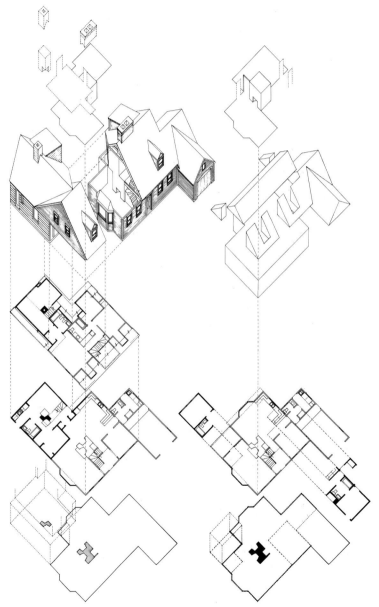

Boguslaw Trondowski, Plan and Axonometric Analysis of Pattern Book Homes

THESIS

Thomas Berge Andersen
MArch I

Via Baltica

The Baltic States became independent in 1991, after years of oppressive Soviet rule. Today they find themselves in a situation where foreign investors are controlling development. One example of this is a highway being planned by the European Community. This road, named Via Baltica, will connect Helsinki in Finland with Warsaw in Poland, passing through the Baltic States. The development occurring along this road is being almost exclusively financed by foreign investors. Local authorities have little or no opportunity to control what is happening and inhabitants are in danger of losing their identity to Central-European Engineers and Planners.

The thesis tries to establish a touchstone or an example for development that will inevitably occur. Investment has already started with service stations and border crossings in order to make the road more efficient. The largest problem to date is the inefficient borders where waiting takes hours or even days.

The thesis naturally focuses on one of the borders. The three countries—Lithuania, Latvia, and Estonia—have three distinct languages and cultures that were ignored by the Soviet authorities, and are partly being treated so now by the European Community.
The site chosen is on the border between Latvia and Estonia. Ainazi, a small fishing village, is the closest neighbor; a place that will be changed forever once the development of the border takes place.

Advisor
Jorge Silvetti with Val Warke

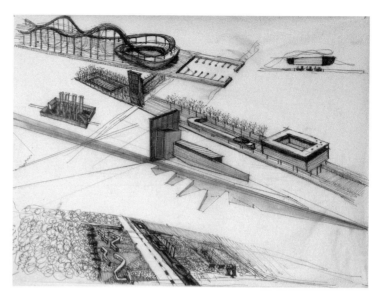

Perspective Views of Site

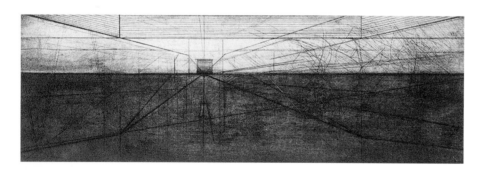

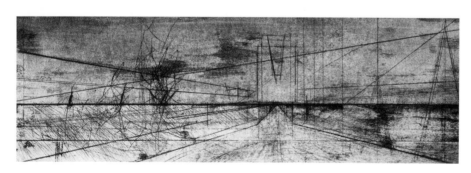

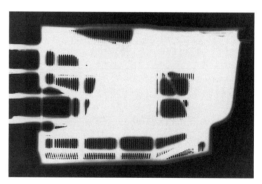

Abstract Study

Site Studies

Paolo Bercah
MArch II

Americah, or, Studies in Architectural Values In the Age of Zeitgeist

Here reviewed by Adolf Loos.

1. Reviewing in 1927 *Towards a New Architecture*, H.R.H.—His Royal Highness/Henry Russell Hitchcock—wrote that "as a theoretician Le Corbusier has stated the problem of the twentieth century architecture; as an artist and a builder he has come near as is perhaps yet possible to the solution of that problem." Some decades later Rem Koolhaas, another theoretician, picked up the pen dropped by Le Corbusier publishing many articles, manifestos, nightmares, and anecdotes whose declared goal is to inform the world about the deliverance of a new creature, Bigness, "a theoretical domain at this fin de siècle." Or, the only thing through which "architecture can dissociate itself from the exhausted artistic/ideological movements of modernism and formalism to regain its instrumentality as vehicle of modernization." Something that made Sanford Kwinter foresee that, sooner or later, "we may well find that, in architecture, the future did in fact begin with Koolhaas." A future depicted in the 1345 pages of his opus magnum standing between us et la fin de siècle.

2. This is believable if one considers that the authors of those theoretical problems/domains and the authors of their solutions are the same. One may think so. But the present reviewer would venture to say that both problems are both absolutely correct and absolutely incorrect at the same time. If the analysis provided seems to be correct, the prophecies derived from there, and driven by the ever-present myth of the Zeitgeist, appear informed by a lesser degree of correctness. One could explain this through analysis of the twentieth century attempting to demystify the terrifying power (seduction?) of this myth. This is the goal of the studies here reviewed. Not influenced by the mentioned theoretical domains, these studies—if the present reviewer is allowed to quote some of the words instead of the drawings provided by the author—are not equipped with "the intention to produce any condensed resume of the century about to die"; and instead they stress how "the obsolescence of an architectural style is a gradual and complex phenomenon, and that the run to modernism happened on a transatlantic scale on the planet after the second world war has extirpated in most cases cultural differences and produced, as a result, amounts of square footage that are greater than any produced in the previous four millennia." After this, the author reminds us that, "unlike in the past, the century about to die (thanks—at least in part—to the myth of the Zeitgeist), will leave, in the forms of cities built ex-novo or of cities indiscriminately enlarged, an image of itself that is much worse than the one it deserves." A case of promises generously delivered au debut de siècle that la fin de siècle can only see as unfulfilled.

3. Undoubtedly, le debut et la fin de siècle as concepts, evocative as they might be, can drive away the imagination of some of its theoreticians. It so happened, one suspects, in the above examples. Luckily, this is not the case of these studies. On the contrary, the studies here reviewed highlight the distance existing between architecture and its "time," and some alternative ways of recording time are easily offered in order to get away from the growing mysticism attached to the year 2000. Having then freed himself from the slavery of the Zeitgeist, the author seems to find something disturbing in the way through which the mentioned domains established an unambiguous relationship between works of architecture and the time—the spirit of the time—in which they are brought into being. As if one were the result of the other. "Yet," the author believes that "architecture has nothing to do with contingency"; that "architecture is a superior value," and, above all, that "it is a-historical." He invites us to "realize that interpreting the architecture of the time purely in terms of contingency means accepting the image its architects wanted to give of themselves as servant fellows of twentieth-century modernism." The author does not hesitate to indicate how "a work of architecture has a historical birth but an a-historical life; a common and universal datum which is the only one that allows architecture to transcend the pretexts that brought it to life: clients, ideologies, le gout et l'ésprit de l'époque." Finally he expresses his belief that "a work of architecture is to be sure a text composed in a specific point in time; it certainly helps us to understand the time and the circumstances in which it was born, but we can by no means exhaust its reasons and arguments with the era of its birth. Quite the contrary, the work of architecture engages different eras, and always in a different way."

4. Because of all this, it should not sound surprising, then, if it so happens that the author of the studies here reviewed believes it is important to find out what a country wanted to be, instead of what it is, or what it was. These studies are the result of that wish, indeed. An intuition that made their author think that the most believable, and therefore the most real, ideas about cities, urbanity, and architectural values—the ones that architects are gently invited to look for in these studies—could be found in a territory named Americah: a figure demanding some attention. Architects' attention. Our attention. Instead of talking of futurology, the author directs his and our interest toward architecture, or, rather, toward "Americah...more or less an ideal figure. Like the Great Gatsby, it has sprung from a 'platonic concept of itself' rather than from any real place."

5. Carried away by the author's enthusiasm not only about the architecture of the past, but also by his attitude toward the future—equipped with the confidence that there are things that only architecture can give us—the present reviewer can only support the positive theory embedded in the studies here reviewed. An attempt to awake in the public a new sensitivity about Americah..."an entity that hides a multitude of profound talents without a program. An entity waiting to be discovered, or rediscovered." Although the theory is not formally presented yet, it seems worthwhile to say that while waiting for this time to come—a time that will equip us with an atlas of it—we have no other choice but to dream about a forthcoming book made of words and not, just for a change, of images. A tale of books, not of everyday worries. A book called "Americah...a design for the whole human race," to allow Fitzgerald to speak, "the last and greatest of all human dreams. Or nothing."

Advisors
George Baird
Homa Fardjadi
Jorge Silvetti

Hilary Bidwell
MLA II

The Entrepreneurial Community

America is ready for new forms of housing. Not an abandonment of the single-family detached house in a yard, but a slow transition from the idealized and isolated unit to a form of development that begins to recognize the changes in lifestyle that much of the population is undergoing. Traditional forms of housing no longer address the needs of the majority of people. And, the traditional form of housing in the United States has become the suburb.

Suburbia is an all-inclusive term for an area predominantly, if not entirely, made up of evenly spaced, single-family detached houses, each on its own lot. This thesis investigates and proposes a form of suburban development designed to meet the needs of a changing society. While maintaining the single-family house, my design establishes a living/working environment with a hierarchical series of open spaces and a network of amenities, transforming the suburban environment into a more communal, productive, and livable space.

The Entrepreneurial Community is made up of a series of residential blocks, the typical block consisting of around twelve single-family lots, each with a detached house and a detached office. The integration of house, office, and garden creates a private indoor/outdoor working and living environment in the backyard, while the integration of office and courtyard garden with other facilities creates a more social and public indoor/outdoor working space.

Advisor
John Stilgoe

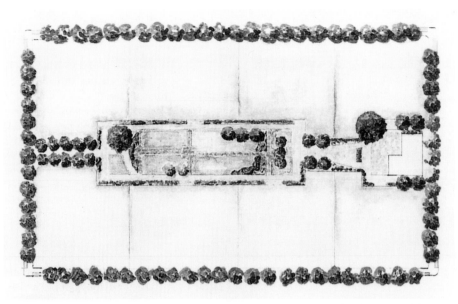

Site Plan: Entrepreneurial Estates

Entrepreneurial Villas

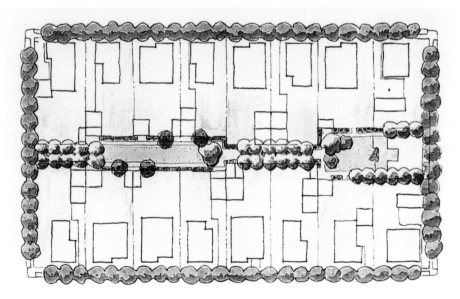

Entrepreneurial Village

Interior View

Eric Russell Bunge
MArch II

Carnival/House:
Soane's Other House

part 1. a video of ALIAS computer animations investigating a fictional, animated architecture.

part 2. a website structured around the ground floor plan of Sir John Soane's house in Lincoln's Inn Fields, London.

Architecture is a spectacle of authority. The carnival is seen in this fictional project as a parallel critique of the spectacle, and as a metaphor for a way of working that temporarily brackets the use in architecture of monological, mediating instruments: the orthogonal projection, and the spatial and temporal fixities of a given program or site.

Soane's house, already a double, already a hyperlinked space, is reinvented as a carnival/house on a website. The merging of two disparate notions—the carnival and the house—is an attempt to import the scale, the inversions, and excesses of the carnival into the familiar domain of the house. The notion of 'house' is thus expanded, as the notion of carnival is compressed.

Within this framework, I speculate on the temporal natures of three types of architectural elements found in the house that construct architectural space in terms of surface, movement and views respectively . The architectural elements— envelope, passage, and picture window—are considered as architectural chronotopes, or elements that have inherent programs. These elements are carnivalized—inverted, doubled and extrapolated—to exaggeration in the hope of revealing these inherent programs and the relationships between them. Soane's extended facade is, for example, renamed as a doubling of envelope. The carnival exaggerations then consist of doubling it again, inverting and continuing the facade to become the thin facade of the ground....

Advisor
Jorge Silvetti

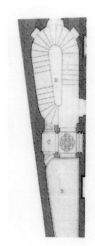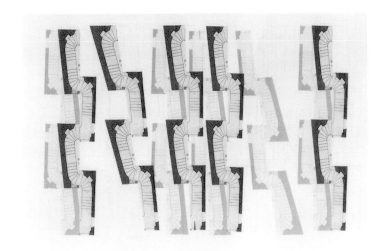

Outer Hall, Inner Hall, Staircase

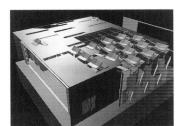

Exterior View: Carnival/House

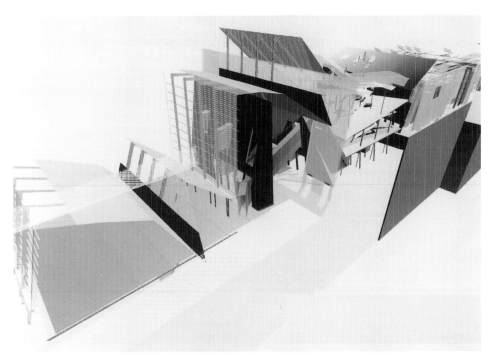

Perspective View: Carnival/House

Alan B. Chun
MArch I

Sento: Ritual Bath

In designing a public bath house for international travelers across the bay from Renzo Piano's Kansai International Airport in Osaka, Japan, this project explores the idea of how the artifice of architecture potentially promotes human ritual and allows such ritual to sustain itself once the momentum of human activity is set into motion.

Although the ritual of public bathing in japan is simple to understand, it confuses many foreigners at first since it involves an elaborate series of steps that follow a specific sequential order (undressing, soaping, rinsing, bathing, massaging, dressing). Although the informality of the bath environment makes the bathing rules appear unimportant, great offense is taken if the steps are not followed in a very particular way (heaven forbid a washcloth be brought into the bathing tanks). In the case of this bath house, the question arises: can architecture really be a catalyst which helps visitors decode and then perform a rital so unfamiliar to them?

By setting up a convincing scene (good story telling) and by coding the building so that potential associations can be made between building and activity (through material combinations, tectonic expression, considerations of conditions of transparency vs. opacity), the building encourages the user to partake in the sensual bathing experience. How the building cogently promotes the complex program was the main focus of this investigation.

Advisor
Ken Kao

Detail of Precedent: Ryonaji Garden

Model View

Aerial View: Structural System

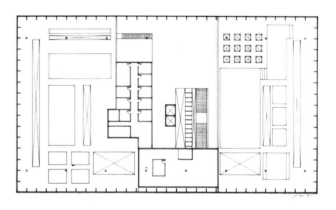

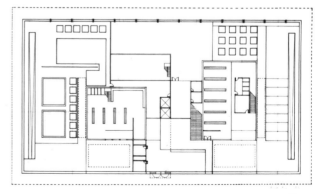

Plans

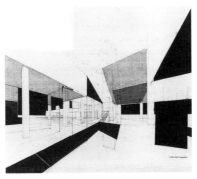

Under-Slab Perspective

F. Jonathan Dreyfous
MArch I

Productions of Thickness: Re-Working High-Rise Public Housing at Alewife

Excavated well into the twentieth-century for brick constructions throughout the Eastern seaboard, a rich seam of clay described a void between the density of Cambridge and the suburban periphery. The Fresh Pond superblocks, completed in 1971 during the last gasp of federally funded high-rise housing, make positive what was once a pit 200 feet deep.

This thesis project carves out new layers of occupation on the ground plane, in the corridor, and within the units. Satellites of programmatic agglomerations (eg. daycare/laundry facilities), as well as "empty" spaces in-between, can produce overlapping trajectories and locate new boundaries within shared spaces. Tethered to the existing vertical cores/structure, corridors are conceived as occupiable linings between the exterior landscape and the reconfigured unit types. Rather than erasing the superblocks, a revised topography emerges as an armature for daily practices, either sanctioned or appropriated. The project attempts to make a open catalog of particular incisions within the generic.

Advisor
Mohsen Mostafavi

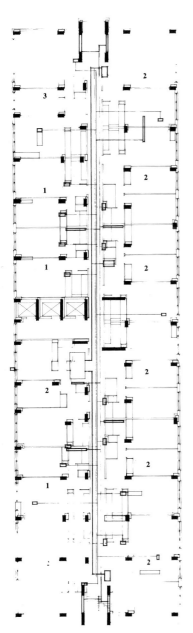

Bones: Vertical Armatures

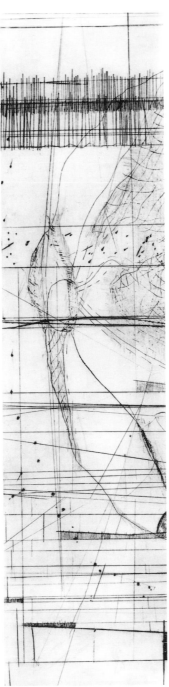

Conceptual Drawing

Conceptual Drawing

View of Existing Apartment Block

John Hong
MArch I

The Space of Translation

If one were to describe the United States as a 'nation,' one would have to be willing to suspend the definition of the word ad infinitum. Suspension as opposed to negation, however, requires a rigorous receptivity that resists closure, and a casting of evidence into relationships that work toward an indeterminate future. Recently the limits of 'nation,' have come to a shattering end. It is no longer possible to construct a morality play between major and minor actors; instead, our 'nation' is a field of intensely overlapping, disjunctive, and oftentimes destructive histories and events.

It is a reinvestigation of the act of translating across these differences that may prove a necessary means of not only navigating these radical disjunctures, but also of narrating cultural practices across linguistic or spatial territorial lines. Like many of the 'ethnic' areas of our cities, Manhattan's Koreatown, located between 28th and 34th Streets east of Broadway, is an area

that places what is marginal and what is 'national' in dialogue—where a particular ethnic group has inscribed its cultural practice onto an inherited urban fabric. Instead of merely examining this kind of urbanity as a diminutive "ghettoization" of the American city, however, the (task of) a translating methodology in Benjaminian terms, is one that would place these cultural transactions in a horizontal, non-hierarchical relationship, where the translation and the 'original' undergo a reciprocating, renewing, as well as maturing, transformation.

Advisor
Mohsen Mostafavi

Model Views

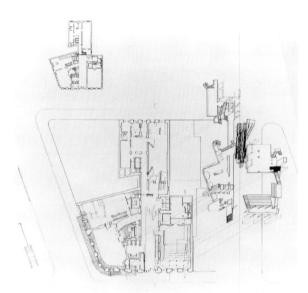

Ground Floor with Mezzanine

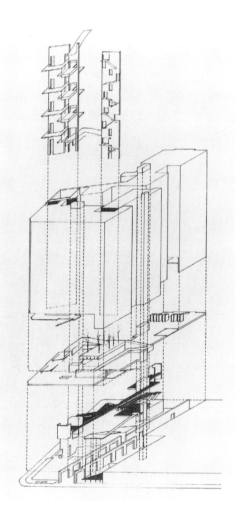

Hotel Martinique Reconfigured

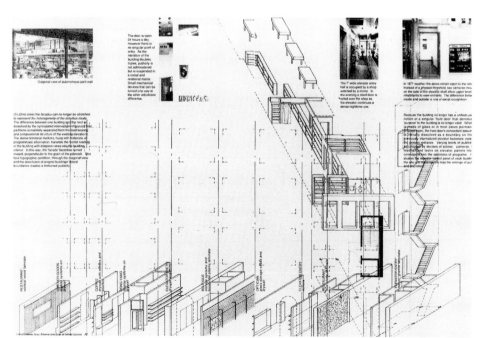

32nd Street Translations

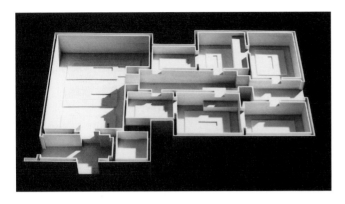

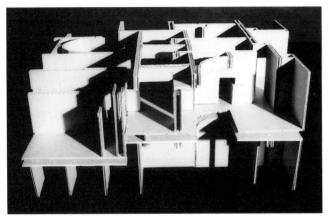

Model Views

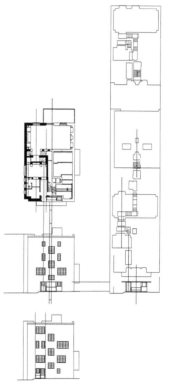

Plan and Sections Showing
Multiple Centers

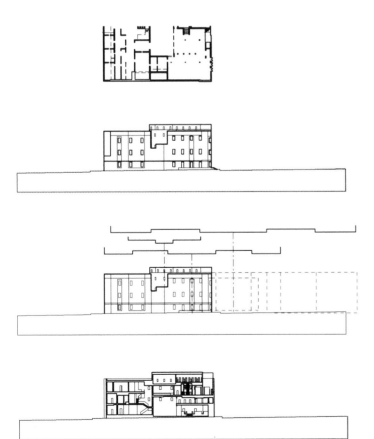

Analytical Sections

Ben Hufford
MArch I

DIS-LOCATION

With the continued dissolution of
a structural language of architecture,
the possibility of any formal meaning is threatened. However, architecture in physical form has not entirely
yielded its critical potential.

This thesis presents a theoretical
approach to critical architecture
utilizing multiple motivating and
constraining systems. An architecture based on pleonastic ordering
systems, outside the singular central
experience of man, has the power to
question the conservative position.

This project for an addition to the
National Portrait Gallery in
Washington, D.C., utilizes identifi-
able structures such as symmetry,
series, and identity to establish
physical conditions of overlap.

The formal structure of the origi-
nal/adjacent Mills Patent Office is
adapted to the constraints of the
new site, with its multiple centers
and boundaries, both real and
implicit. As these conditions produce multiple physical conditions
occupying a single space, the work
is to negotiate the artifacts left by
the generative mechanisms. Such
negotiation of the conditions is not
premised on resolution, but on
allowing the difficulties of the motivating conditions to remain in the
final configuration. True to the
notion that a homocentric understanding of a single absolute truth
is impossible, an architecture that is
a physical manifestation of the difficulties of arbitrary hierarchy systems
may be both revealing and positive.

Advisor
Preston Scott Cohen

Richard Jones
MArch II

Of Object and Field

In a lecture he [Aalto] said: 'I have a feeling that there are too many cases in life where the organization of things is experienced as too brutal. The architect's task is to make our life patterns more sympathetic.' Good architecture therefore alleviates; it removes and smoothes out the unpleasant roughness of sensation. If this orientation were pursued to its limit, building would disappear not by realizing the dream of dematerialization that enthralled so many other modern architects, but by receding into the background of perception, enabling human activity by following its varied courses without ever getting in the way.

Robin Evans, *The ProjectiveCast,* 1995

The differentiation between the discrete architectural object and the field in which it lies has become too distinct. This has resulted in an urban landscape of disassociated, self-referential objects and conditions that can only contribute to the alienation of people from their environment.

The answer to this problem does not lie in the proposal of a homogenizing tendency in the design of our cities and architecture. Rather, as this proposal suggests, inconspicuousness can both blur the distinction of object and field, and simultaneously recognize the disjunction between the two. Such a practice results in the seeming inconspicuousness of the object in relation to its field at first glance. Further investigation however, reveals the experience to be something more, and reveals a celebration of the disjunction between object and field.

The vehicle for the investigation of this problem was an addition to the Fine Arts Department at the University of Kentucky. Four methods began to recur throughout the design process. First, a depth of site was emergent. This was a consideration of the site at many levels, physically and conceptually. Second, methods of fragmentation were investigated to help implement a blurring of building and site. Third, an attempt to collapse the individual and the experience of the architecture was researched through a method of peripatetic movement. Last, these three practices combine to create a continuum, which both blurs and reveals the relationship of building and site.

Advisor
Wilfried Wang

Model View

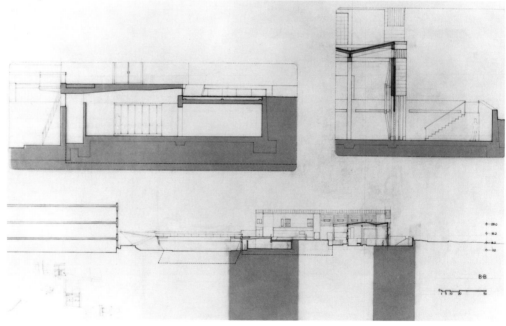

Sections

Road Studies

Valise

Gwynne Keathley
MArch I

Behind the Curtain Wall: Shifting Equilibrium at the Cherry Lane Theatre, New York, NY

This thesis develops a methodological approach—constructing urbanity and domesticity in ways that are not mutually exclusive but rather are mutually supportive. Specifically, it uses the notion of the uncanny to shift the conventional equilibrium between public and private to make public space that is not anti-intimate and private space that is not anti-urban(e). Its strategy takes advantage of peculiarities of scale and the temporality of events to create conditions in the urban realm that oscillate between the privacy associated with the home and the externality/publicity associated with the city. [see diagram]

The renovation of the Cherry Lane Theatre shifts the equilibrium of the residential West Greenwich Village block by alternately emptying and filling residential and institutional spaces to bring forward both the suppressed presence of the theatre and the hidden history of the site. The project carves out the spaces of the theatre and fills the Bedford Mews courtyard with the addition of a Winter Garden theatre that fills the courtyard and doubles as an intermission space and residential garden. A curtain wall, a tease of construction and interior finishes, both conceals the institutional events of the Winter Garden and supports its building. Here the curtain, while recalling both theatre and home, maintains the privacy of the residences and the intrigue of the theatre behind it. A new theatre wall inserted in the 3-1/2-foot-wide gap between the theatre (former stable) and the adjacent residence doubles as backstage and overflow balconies for the audience. Finally, the 8-1/2-foot-wide Edna St. Vincent Millay reading room doubles her original house width at 75 1/2 Bedford Street, creating a light well for the new entrance to the Cherry Lane Theatre. The reading room fills a hay-hoisting gap between a former stable and the residence and recalls the history of the theatre initiated by Millay.

Advisor
Linda Pollak

Model View: Unroofed

Sectional Model View

Strange Scales

Alt Reality

Villa Bosc

Anne Marie Lubrano
MArch I

The Horizon of Knowledge: A Branch Library for Morningside Heights

As a native of Brooklyn, this investigation began as an observation made upon my return from the northwestern plains of Wyoming to the city of New York. By comparison, the dense urban context of New York does not allow for the expansive landscape of Wyoming; the city is lost without a horizon. In order to keep the urban condition from closing in on itself and from remaining a location of cluttered placelessness, my thesis began as an attempt to define and construct the realm of the horizon. This desire made the selection of the square, flat Manhattan site at 113th street and Broadway (a particularly dense and viewless corner) an easy decision. Located next-door to Columbia University, the site had long been proposed as a location for a much needed branch library for the forgotten public of Morningside Heights.

The program of a library functions in a similar manner to the horizon. From a literary sense the horizon marks the edge of the known world, the collapse of all human knowledge and experience into a thick line. The horizon line orders this information, separating the imaginable world (the realm of the known) from the world of the sublime (the realm beyond imagination of the terrific). The library is a building that marks the boundary between the physical realm (the three-dimensional book or the printed word) and the mental realm of the imagination. It is a place that is occupied physically, but abandoned mentally. At the library, the reader defies the constructed boundary and extends the limits of the physical built container to the limits of the imagination, toward the line of the horizon. This notion of a physically solid yet mentally permeable boundary is the concept that shaped the detail of the interior skin of the building.

The detail illustrates a piece of the browsing wall. The thin layer of unfinished steel panels lines the facade and shades books from direct exposure to the light. At points in the wall system, large folded panels capped with wood reveal small apertures of light and create individual book stands. The varying heights of the folded panels allow the average adult, young adult, and child to stand and read with the awareness of a space beyond the facade, but do not permit direct exterior views. Hence, an extension of physical and mental space occurs concurrently.

The modular 16-gauge steel panels, based on the maximum size of a book, are folded to achieve maximum strength and stability. As seen in section, the construction of the panels corresponds to that of the bookshelves. The panels are bolted between 1/4" steel ribs that rest on the structural steel beams visible in the elevation. The entire system is fastened in place with bolts for ease of assembly at minimum expense. The unfinished steel mimics the erratic unpredictable, multi-layered imaginative process of the mind.

The two layers that create the elevation, the interior of steel and the exterior of glass, reinforce the idea of collapse and aid in the efficiency of the wrapper of the building. The actual facade is a double paned glass curtain that physically separates the building from the street, yet allows for the fluid exchange of light to occur. This desired character of the facade is explored in my black and white print from January '96. This work is an attempt to explore the physical depth of the horizon. As light refracts and bends to reveal and define the spaces of the sublime, this print most closely realizes the effect that the steel browsing wall is intended to create. By day, the shadowy halls of the book stacks are splintered with light, while at night the facade glows with the tiny eruptions of light; both events approach the sublime quality illustrated in the print.

Advisor
Toshiko Mori

Browsing Wall

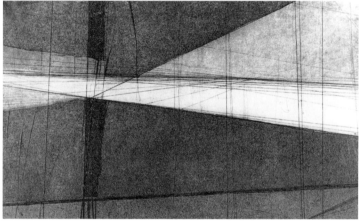

Conceptual Drawing: Horizon V

Model View

Model View: At Night

Regional Land Use Analysis
Potential Aquaculture Areas

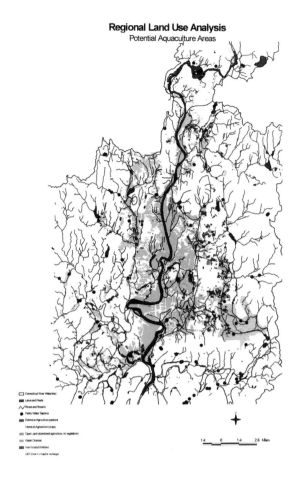

□ Connecticut River Watershed
■ Lakes and Ponds
∧ Rivers and Streams
● Public Water Supplies
■ Extensive Agriculture pasture
Intensive Agriculture crops
Open Land abandoned agriculture, no vegetation
Waste Disposal
Non-forested Wetlands
DEP Zone II Aquifer recharge

1.4   0   1.4   2.8 Miles

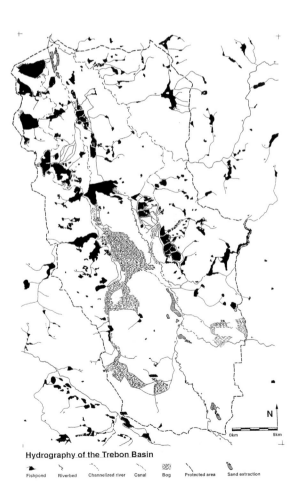

Hydrography of the Trebon Basin

Fishpond   Riverbed   Channelized river   Canal   Bog   Protected area   Sand extraction

N

0km   5km

Martin Mildbrandt
MLA II

A Study of Sustainable Aquaculture in the Trebon Basin and its Application to the Connecticut River Valley

This thesis investigates a model of sustainable aquaculture from the Trebon Basin in the Czech Republic, a landscape that has been intensively used by human populations for 600 years and where the hydrology and natural species composition of the original ecosystem have been completely transformed. The Trebon Basin is analyzed at a regional and site-specific scale to understand the evolution, design, function, and management of the fishponds. Through an understanding of design and management techniques, principles of sustainability are distilled and applied to a case study in the Connecticut River Valley in Massachusetts.

In the Trebon Basin, centuries of human intervention, settlement, and production via channelization and excavation did not create a landscape of habitat destruction and species extinction. In fact, sustainable design and management techniques have enhanced the biodiversity and productivity of this landscape over time. Today, the mosaic of fishponds and narrow dams is dotted with nature reserves and laced together with a network of interpretive and recreational trails, effectively synthesizing production, nature protection, and recreation.

The second section of the thesis explores the possibility of applying principles of aquaculture design proven to be sustainable in the Trebon Basin to a section of the Connecticut River Valley in western Massachusetts. The intention is not to duplicate the Czech system but rather to explore the possibility of integrating some of the desirable principles of sustainability and multiple-use into a uniquely American industry with great growth potential.

The river basin study area in western Massachusetts is flat and comprised of glacial lakebed deposits of sand and gravel, creating a high water table. Agriculture is predominant and there are a number of existing aquaculture facilities within the study area due to the availability and quality of water. The case-study focuses on Red Wing meadow Trout Farm and Bioshelter, an aquaculture facility since 1984. The design proposal of this thesis involves the expansion of fish production capability by 100 percent at Red Wing Meadow in a manner that also enhances wildlife habitat, and is economically, hydrologically, and ecologically sustainable.

Advisors
Carl Steinitz
Anita Berrizbeitia
Michael Binford

Aerial View of Site

Pantelis Papadopoulos
MArch I

Nicosia: Multiple Realities

This study addresses 'site' as a palimpsest, where urban space is inhabited by both acknowledging the desire for permanence and recognizing the fact of impermanence. Site is examined in terms of the historical events and the variables of ethnicity that have altered its look, use, and occupation by marking an internal structure through displacement and misuse. This internal structure allows and makes visible the layering and superimposition of existing programs with images of suggested programs.

The old city of Nicosia is the site of study. Due to its division, the city embodies conditions of displacement, misuse, and abandonment that have caused a loss of its cultural identity. They have also created the need for an internal structure based on the several layers of occupation and use that are so particular to the place.

An architecture and program are proposed through which the multiple realities present on the site will become evident in the various uses and levels of occupation of its space. The project creates moments that are 'strange' as a strategy to enter into the site itself. This 'strangeness' is brought forth through the mapping of movement, views, sound, and their proximities to the various political, cultural, and economic borders found throughout the site. In turn the building's form and programmatic content is seen as an analog to the various site conditions.

The building occupies the whole site. The boundaries of construction correspond to the distinct enclosures of different states of movement around the site. The building surrounds and constructs the form of the meeting places and places the form in contact with the movement of the city.

The ways in which an identity can be revealed through an architectural form that is neither articulated hierarchically nor programmatically distinguishable, becomes very important.

Advisor
Homa Fardjadi

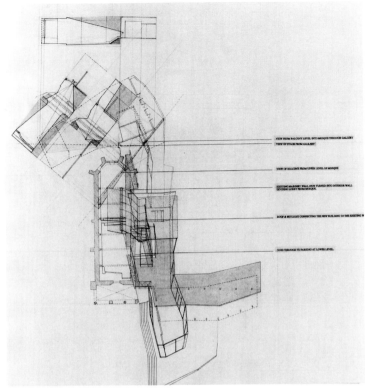

Encounters, Adjacencies, Visual Connections

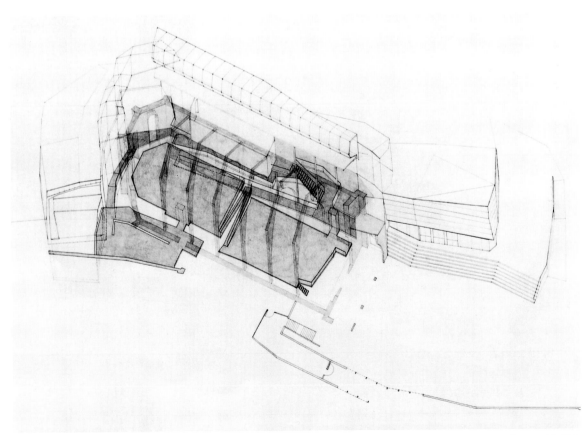

Axonometric View

Hillary Quarles
MLA I

PARTICIPATORY TOURISM:
The Exploration of a Changing Landscape on the Taraco Peninsula of Lake Titicaca, Bolivia

Tourism is one of the fastest growing industries across the globe. To many small communities throughout the world, money from tourism is critical to the local economy. But these communities have paid the price of environmental and cultural degradation. In *Preserve or Destroy: Tourism and the Environment* (1995), Jonathan Croall relates that "Tourism at its worst has caused overcrowding, damage to the physical environment, conflicts within communities, increased crime and prostitution, traffic congestion and pollution, and an incalculable amount of inappropriate development in some of the world's most beautiful regions." As people have become aware of this degradation, tourists have demanded environmentally sensitive tours and the industry has responded with the concept of "ecotours."

Ecotourism is defined as ecologically sensitive tourism that both educates tourists about the natural environment and furthers conservation. If successful, it can create economic opportunities for the local people that give the community a strong incentive to practice good stewardship over their natural resources. However, in practice, ecotourism has not reached these goals. Exotic habitats that attract tourists are often too fragile to withstand their own popularity. Remote regions, such as the Himalayas, are now so accessible that mountains are deforested by trekkers seeking campwood. Moreover, travel agencies have bypassed local communities by providing ecotours directly out of cities thus denying rural residents the ability to reap benefits from the surrounding resources. Ultimately, the ideals of ecotourism are thwarted.

This thesis investigation attempts to redefine traditional concepts of tourism through the creation of a new tourism based on participation. In *participatory tourism* the tourist is introduced into the landscape through a series of activities and experiences that reveal its culture, history, and ecology through participation rather than observation. The continued success of participatory tourism depends on the ability of local resources to absorb visitors into cycles of life and change. Therefore, basic development, such as lodging, circulation, and signage must be limited; it must be inspired by the language and form of the landscape as it exists now and it must be able to change and evolve over time.

A prototypical plan for participatory tourism has been developed for the Taraco Peninsula of Lake Titicaca, Bolivia. It proposes a modest system of circulation, lodging, and tourist services. It develops a series of activities that gives structure to the tourist experience and ties it to the local population. It demonstrates a prototypical approach and process to the introduction of tourist facilities in the landscape by linking form to seasonal and evolutionary change. Using photographs, drawings, digital imagery, and maps, the plan describes ways that visitors can participate in the landscape and culture with limited impact on resources.

The final test of the plan is the test of time. What would happen if tourism suddenly stopped due to a local revolution or a global crisis? What would happen over the span of one or many years? Life for the Aymara on the Taraco Peninsula would resume as it has for the past century, but there would be another layer of residue on the land. Like the Tiwanaku, and the Inca and the Spanish that came before them, tourism would leave its telltale docks, a layer of green gravel, and renovated buildings. The Aymara would incorporate these forms into their local lives: the docks would be used to land their boats and gather totora, the lodging would be used by the Mother's Club for its monthly meeting or by the local community to house an artisan school, and the tourist centers would turn into small stores or restaurants. The Aymara would miss the additional income from tourism, but the roads would remain paved and the wells would bring clean water. The brief period of wealth would be incorporated into their lives and into the land itself. Eventually tourism would return and the Aymara would again teach foreigners how to weave, how to live within the landscape, and how to conceptualize their lives around the lifecycle of a potato. Some of the interventions would resurface as part of the tourist circuit while others would be forgotten in the evolution of the landscape.

Unlike typical tourism development, participatory tourism enables the forms and organization of development to be dictated by the local culture and environment rather than by the preconceived ideals of foreign investors. It creates viable economic opportunities with limited development funding simply by analyzing the natural and cultural resources and by creating a plan based on the existing organization of the landscape.

Advisor
Michael Binford

Kevin L. Rice
MArch I

The Standard and the Particular

The concepts of the *Standard* and the *Particular* are most often presented as dialectical concepts; the standard always opposed to the unruly particular, the particular always opposed to the oppressive standard. I would argue, however, that these concepts are inseparable concepts that should be dealt with together and not as opposing elements. Their true value to architecture may lie in the concurrent exploration of these concepts and the fine line that simultaneously separates and joins them. I am interested in an architecture where what is standard and what is particular to the architecture remains unclear.

In the design of this school, I have taken the prototype program for elementary schools from the Houston Independent School District and brought that to a mixed neighborhood in Houston. Through the use of both standardized construction materials (the Butler™ framing system, Hardiplank™ siding, storefront glazing, etc.), and more particular components (shading devices, cabinetry, etc.) that can be built by light industrial shops in the neighborhood I have attempted to evoke the quality of the site as well as the expectations of the program.

Advisor
Wilfried Wang

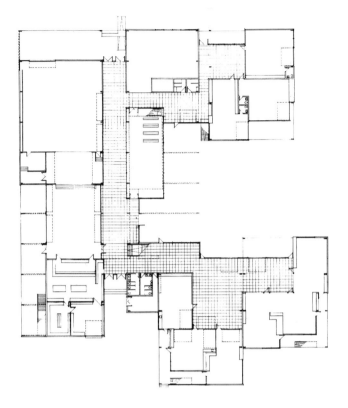

Plan and Elevation of Proposed School

Interior Model View

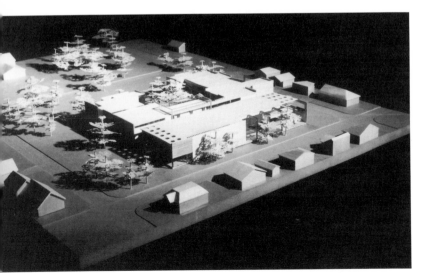

Site Model View

Elena Salij
MArch I

Groundruled Double

This project—a proposal for a new Fenway Park, on a waterfront site in the Fort Point Channel area of Boston—seeks to investigate the form of public spaces in the city, and the obligations conferred on those who dare to rebuild or replace monuments.

The project arises from the conceptualization of the ballpark form as the product of negotiation between incompatible external *and* internal pressures, both literal and metaphoric. The external pressures—the location of surrounding streets, a small and inhospitably figured site, the need to orient the building to approaches and views—are considerable, and pertain to almost any large-scale construction in a mature city. The internal pressures—the orientation and dimension of the playing field as dictated by the rules of major league baseball, as well as the expectations of the fans for an intimate and inviting space, and of the owners for a large and profitable park—are particular to the highly idiosyncratic program of this ballpark, but are similarly inflexible. The principal architecture of the project, the building that houses the seats, the circulation, and the commercial areas of the park, must absorb and reconcile these pressures while maintaining a kind of logic and integrity. The result is a figure that bears the marks of its formation: the wracks, sheers, folds, and pleats that remember the process of making, and are an homage to the original Fenway Park.

Advisor
Preston Scott Cohen

Model Views of Proposed Stadium

Yoshiko Sato
MArch II

New Structuring: Housing and Urbanism in Kobe

In the vast destructive aftermath of the Great Hanshin Earthquake of January 17, 1995, the imperative for this thesis was to define the reconstruction of Kobe through the establishment of a dynamic equilibrium and optimum interdependency between housing and urban scale propositions in the Nagato district. The ontological questions of the thesis—housing and urbanism in Kobe—while acknowledging international influence and developments, are founded upon the regions specific geologic, structural, and temporal criteria and the sociocultural manifestations that are unique to the evolution of Japanese cities, spatial and tectonic typologies. The architectural proposition is determined and delineated in the horizontal and vertical section, from multiple vantage points and scales, balancing addition with uncovering, revealing both the natural and the constructed, public and private spaces within the intended horizontal thickening of the urban fabric.

The primary urban intervention mediates the potential realignment of the collapsed east/west transportation infrastructure as an interchange/building/landscape. The structure provides the community with a programmatic mixed-use facility of parking, civic, commercial, and recreational activities, while seeking to reinstate the former topography and urban morphology along the bisecting river as "reflected" ground. The housing's internal organization and external description are woven into the intermediate scale infrastructure and parks with networks of pedestrian circulation. The district is integrated with the greater city through terrains of undulating horizontal surfaces and the infusion of mixed-income residents and regional economic development.

The housing and urban propositions, together with phenomenological, social, and cultural considerations, are structurally and spatially determined for seismic loading. In light of the recent disaster, special attention is given to the provision of water and shelter in the event of a future emergency relief situation.

Advisor
José Rafael Moneo

Site Plan

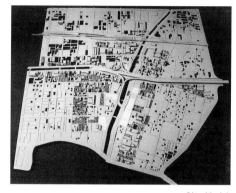

Site Model

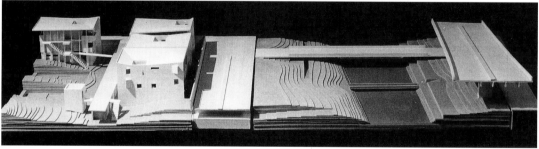

Model View: Detail of Site with Housing Units

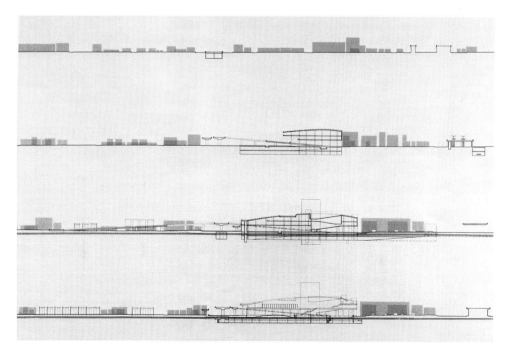

Site Sections Through Urban Intervention to Housing Complex

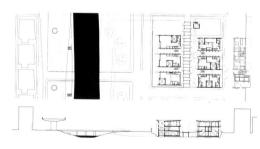

Plan and Site Section of Housing Complex

George J. Schafer
MArch 1

Language of the Architect: Descriptions of Architectural Discourse

No answer in words can reply to a question of things.
                    Ralph Waldo Emerson

Speak, so that I may see.
                    Socrates

Because the architectural profession is a social practice, architects must use words and drawings to communicate their ideas. This has always been the case. It only stands to reason, then, that architects, regardless of which mode of expression they prefer, should want to understand exactly how verbal and visual languages work together and against each other, so that ideas can be communicated in the most effective manner.

Buildings are silent. Drawings and models are silent representations of buildings. It is an ironic aspect of architectural education that in order to be able to open up a way to come at these silent entities we talk all day long in school, and try to find ways to pitch the workings of our mind toward these absolutely wordless embodiments of thought. What we do in the architectural jury, in fact, is attempt to relate two very distinct realms of operation: the silent and the spoken.

A central argument of this thesis is that the relationship between verbal language and visual language, as it exists in the everyday experience of the architectural jury, is much more complex than is evident in a simple dichotomy between two opposite forms of communication. Because of this, any discussion of architectural discourse needs to be as layered as the discourse itself. Just as there are many different types of drawings, each with one or more purposes (whether to aid in the process of conceptualization or to explain or present architectural ideas), there are also variations in verbal discourse.

Empirical data collected specifically for this study using audiotapes of architectural juries uncovers the varying modalities of verbal language: how words function in the discourse, and how they can affect the reading of the drawings and models. Situational language attempts to frame the reading of the visual presentation by providing descriptions of process, program, and meaning within the range of drawings and models. Referential language is used to orient and emphasize drawings and specific information within them. Incidental language acts to structure the shifts between the different modalities, and indicates a continuous process whereby students and critics attempt to position themselves with regard to their respective assumptions. The drawings and models create a situation in which each of these modalities is necessary for a productive discourse. Therefore, any discussion of the representation and communication of architectural ideas should include equal consideration of words and drawings.

Presently, architects view each type of communication as a discrete and separate entity; they deal with verbal and visual languages as competing discourses. This segregation of words and images may be inherently tied to the idea of presentation itself (as it exists in the jury setting), as well as the difference between process and presentation drawings.

If we were to look at any number of initial process-sketches drawn by architects or by students, we would see alongside the drawn image words and phrases that verbally articulate ideas within the sketch. Words, in this stage of design, most often act as reminders of important ideas central to the architect's thinking. The drawn image, then, acts as a visual parallel to these ideas. Verbal and visual languages appear in this instance as two forms of description working toward the same goal. Equally important is the fact that they occupy the same space: the paper.

The same cannot be said of presentation drawings. Rarely do final drawings contain words, and if they do include written text, it is generally perfunctory labeling and designation (as in notes on construction documents, titles, etc.). The design process, if seen as the transformation from the sketch to the presentation drawing, also embodies the transformation of the words on the sketch into a visual image. In other words, what begins as words and images on the same page evolves into image alone.

The absence of words (which embody ideas and attempt to represent in the same way the image does) on the presentation drawing places a distance between verbal and visual language. In the jury setting, the words take the form of verbal communication, and as such the gap between words and images becomes not only theoretical, but spatial; it is represented by the physical distance between the designer and his or her drawings. No longer do words and images occupy the same page. The problem with this distance is that once one separates words and images, one can begin to think about them separately.

This separation in our thinking, however, is antithetical to the communication of architectural ideas because the drawing rarely stands alone. The findings of this empirical study reveal that the drawings and models in the visual presentation within the jury setting are unable to effectively communicate in the discourse in the absence of many types of verbal description.

Referential language seems to indicate that drawings need to be designated directly in order to be understood. Even the most conventional types of drawings, those drawings that architects are taught to "read"—plans, sections, elevations, and details, etc.—can contain a multitude of information. Referential language is used to emphasize those things that are primary to the expression of the designer's ideas. Without this verbal designation, architects, in the discursive situation, are forced to rely on a base of knowledge that may not be shared by everyone and which is usually not adequate for an understanding of the specifics of each project. Further, there are often drawings and models that are the product of processes that are either personal or complex. Often these types of drawings fall outside of our base of shared knowledge, and as a result require verbal description to contribute in the discourse.

Although not directly related to the visual presentation, situational language is also necessary for the understanding of drawings and models. There is often the assumption that ideas should be present in all forms of visual representation. Rarely, however, are these ideas explicitly communicated in the absence of their verbal articulation. Transcripts recorded at architectural juries suggest that critics are often unable to engage visual material unless it has been framed within a verbal idea statement. In its absence, critics are forced to rely on assumptions that might not be shared by the student, which often leads to interpretations that rarely coincide with the intentions of the design.

The presence of both types of language in the discourse—referential and situational—illustrates the predicament architects find themselves in with respect to their belief in the ability of drawings and models to communicate architectural ideas; they represent an oscillation between our faith in the drawing, and the realization that visual images often fall short of our expectations.

Situational language, because it gives the drawing a space to "speak for itself" in the discourse, is the direct result of our faith in it as a means of expression. This faith is certainly justifiable, given the amount of time architects labor over drawings and models. What might take ten seconds to describe verbally can often take days of making to represent visually. It stands to reason, then, that we would want these visual objects to do more than just act as ends in themselves. We believe that drawings must communicate, and this is one reason why architects put so much energy into their making.

Advisor
Ed Robbins

Craig Shillitto
MArch II

De-familiarization:
An Arrival Center Adjacent to
the Washington Monument

It was the intent of this thesis to identify the term "de-familiarization" by researching and defining its modes of operation. In the preparatory thesis a matrix of collaged domestic objects developed a methodology whereby common objects and conditions are re-sensitized by additive interpretations instigated through an artist/architect's insertion.

Research of the Washington Monument site illuminated the common mythologized elements as well as subtle incongruencies. The Arrival Center program locates a large cube (measuring 96 feet in all dimensions) in the presently unmarked center of the Washington Mall. The marking of the cross-axis confronts the Washington Monument's misalignment orienting the visitor from the position of center. Visitors by subway, and through extensive underground bus and autoparking structures, emerge beneath the center from the mound that the Washington Monument rests on.

The original Robert Mills monument design embodied a democratic principle within the European obelisk. As with the arrival center, visitors would occupy the position of center looking out rather than looking up at a single foci. The Washington Monument as a simple geometric obelisk is singularly understood. Its multiplicity is not a question of form but rather a dialogue of the obelisk's physical, historical, and cultural adjacency to other places and events. By contrast, the Arrival Center exterior attempts to be a monument with no singular reading. It exists at a suitable scale and material to let it appropriately occupy the mall. The concrete louvered facades change with relation to the movement and distance of the viewer. Within an architectural strategy of adjacency are located quotidian elements with views and fragments of the familiar and mythologized Washington, D.C.

Advisor
Rodolphe el-Khoury

Section Through Arrival Center and Monument

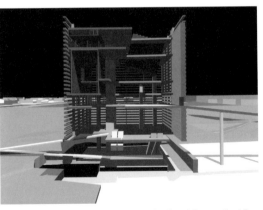

Sectional Perspective View

Aerial View of Site Looking South

Interior View of Garage

J. Cordell Steinmetz
MArch I

If we call this multifarious between the world then the world is the house, which is inhabited by mortals. The single houses however, the villages, the cities, are works of architecture, which in and around themselves gather the multifarious between. The buildings bring the earth as the inhabited landscape cvlose to man and at the same time place the nearness of neighborly dwelling under the expanse of the sky.
Martin Heidegger

Man's need to make sense of his environment is a primordial condition. Whenever and however man was initially thrust into this world, he was simultaneously cosseted and confronted by that which surrounded him. Instigated by that imperative, its cold rain and snow, he had pressing need to understand it. Geometry is an artifact of that need. In order to reach an understanding of his environment, he has abstracted both himself and

Interior View of Sanctuary

the landscape, performing an internal calculus relating the two, understanding an external presence through an internal consciousness. He has also created a totalizing matrix within which the act of building becomes necessary.

In abstracting himself in order to understand his environment, he has established two components of a possible dialogue. Man and the landscape, through their abstraction, however, remain only tenuously related. There remains a need for mediation, for the explication of a deeper relationship. Building becomes that mediator, giving substance to abstraction. If man and the landscape are to become parts of a meaningful whole, clearly, building on the landscape—constructing man's stationary proxy—needs to externally mediate the seeming discrepancy of man and the landscape. Building, in its being in the

landscape *and* above the horizon (approaching the sky), makes it possible for him to observe through the constructed metaphor of the building, the nature of his own place In the world, 'Landscape Is a space where human life takes place. It Is ... a *lived space* between earth and sky." (Christian Norberg-Schulz *Perspecta* 20). Building, in its multivalent presence negotiates this 'between.' In its presence in the landscape, in delimiting space, building actively engages both earth and sky Into a dialogue. Finally, in building's engagement with the sky, while in the ground (building's inherent both/and condition), as man's stationary proxy, it extemalizes not only the relationship between man and the landscape but also man's relationship with the sky. Building, then, allows for a deep understanding of the interrelationship among man, earth, and the heavens. A gestalt is established.

The site of St. Peter's of the Wall is a cornfield on the southern edge of South Bend, Indiana. It is bounded on its North and West by tract housing. To its South and East lie cornfields. The parish compound consists of a church, cemetery, stations of the cross, CCD (religious education) building, rectory and parish offices, parking, and maintenance shed. The compound is aligned alongside a knoll that runs West-East (the historic orientation of a church). An XY grid is reinserted into the center of the site. The sanctuary culminates one axis, the cemetery and horizon the other. There is cleft in the knoll, inscribing the reinsertion of the grid.

Advisor
Jonathan Levi

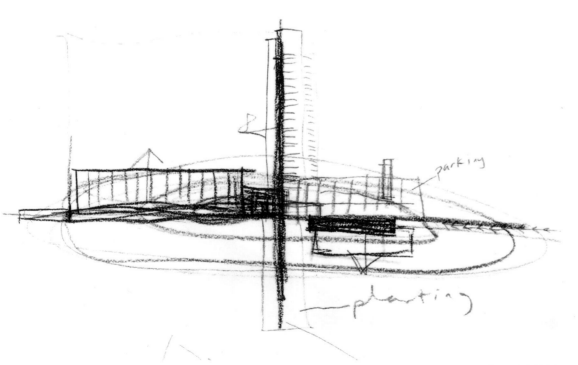

Conceptual Sketch

May Tin Sung
MArch I

Beijing Housing

This thesis evolved from a series of investigations into Chinese domestic culture as represented in pre-Communist, Communist, and contemporary housing situations. Through Chinese architectural articles and other Chinese housing experts, I was able to compile a catalogue of different domestic representations of these periods. In comparison, the original urban setting of the Ming Dynasty was less altered by the Communist government than that of the contemporary Socialist government under a new consumerist culture. The commune approach of the 1950s continues the growth of the original fabric in domestic and urban situations. However, in contemporary Beijing, the new approach is one of renewal, focussing on ways of rebuilding and new construction, that are neither nostalgic nor in the "style" of American suburban developments. The results are the relocation of the original inhabitants and the destruction of the city's fabric.

The phenomenon of highrise housing projects overshadowing the typical vernacular courtyard houses is a common sight in today's Beijing, and, indeed, is the case my chosen site in the west city. The design intention is to mediate between the super-building blocks and the existing courtyard structures. Through an understanding of existing program on the site, institutional, industrial, educational, and commercial programs for a childcare center, a light-industrial facility, and a market were set up to welcome the new entrepreneurial industries. The density and quality of housing were also increased to accommodate new concepts of private ownership. Thus new housing types will accommodate new social clients such as single persons, multi-generational families, and nuclear families.

Advisor
Peter Rowe

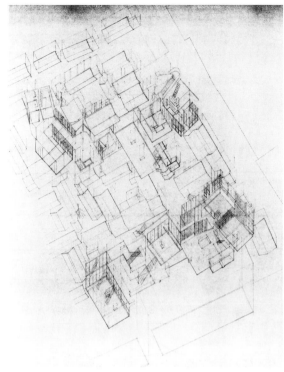

Axonometric View

Perspective View of Courtyard Between Housing Blocks

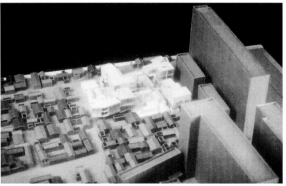

Site Model View

Faculty of Design
1995-96

Peter G. Rowe

Dean of the Faculty of Design

*Raymond Garbe Professor of
Architecture and Urban Design*

ARCHITECTURE

Emeriti

Gerhard Kallmann
Professor of Architecture Emeritus

Eduard Sekler
*Professor of Architecture and Osgood Hooker
Professor of Visual Art Emeritus*

Jerzy Soltan
*Nelson Robinson, Jr., Professor of Architecture
and Urban Design Emeritus*

Academic and Adjunct Faculty

George Baird
Professor of Architecture

Carole Bolsey
Lecturer in Architecture

Carol Burns
Associate Professor of Architecture

Howard Burns
*Robert and Marion Weinberg Professor
of the History of Architecture*

Preston Scott Cohen
Associate Professor of Architecture

Homa Fardjadi
Associate Professor of Architecture

Darell Fields
Assistant Professor of Architecture

K. Michael Hays
Professor of Architectural Theory

Jacques Herzog
Arthur Rotch Design Critic in Architecture

Kenneth Kao
Lecturer in Architecture

Sheila Kennedy
Associate Professor of Architecture

Rem Koolhaas
*Professor in Practice of Architecture and
Urban Design*

Sarah Williams Ksiazek
Assistant Professor of Architectural History

Jude LeBlanc
Assistant Professor of Architecture

William LeMessurier
Adjunct Professor of Architectural Technology

Jonathan Levi
Design Critic in Architecture

Malcolm McCullough
Associate Professor of Architecture

Pierre de Meuron
Arthur Rotch Design Critic in Architecture

Enric Miralles
Design Critic in Architecture

José Rafael Moneo
Josep Lluis Sert Professor of Architecture

Toshiko Mori
Professor in Practice of Architecture

Mohsen Mostafavi
Associate Professor of Architecture

Linda Pollak
Assistant Professor of Architecture

Spiro N. Pollalis
Professor of Design Technology

Chris Risher, Jr.
Design Critic in Architecture

Peter Rose
Adjunct Professor of Architecture

Carl M. Sapers
*Adjunct Professor of Studies in Professional
Practice in Architecture*

Daniel Schodek
Kumagai Professor of Architectural Technology

Mack Scogin
Kajima Adjunct Professor of Architecture

John Seiler
*Adjunct Professor of Architecture and
Urban Design*

Jorge Silvetti
*Nelson Robinson, Jr., Professor of Architecture,
and Chair, Department of Architecture*

Christine Smith
Professor of Architectural History

Albert Szabo
*Professor of Architecture and Osgood Hooker
Professor of Visual Art*

Wilfried Wang
Design Critic in Architecture

James Williamson
Assistant Professor of Architecture

Visiting Faculty

Mark Angelil
Alan Balfour
Frederick Fisher
Richard Gluckman
Sarah Graham
Kimo Griggs
Jeffrey Inaba
Carlos Jimenez
George Liaropoulos-Legendre
Brian MacKay-Lyons
Sandro Marpillero
Larry Mitnick
Eric Owen Moss
João António Mota
Nick Musso
John Patkau
Patricia Patkau
Monica Ponce de Leon
Hashim Sarkis
Rafael Viñoly
Jane Wernick